Advances in Instructional Technology

George H. Voegel, *Editor*
William Rainey Harper College

NEW DIRECTIONS FOR COMMUNITY COLLEGES
ARTHUR M. COHEN, *Editor-in-Chief*
FLORENCE B. BRAWER, *Associate Editor*

Number 55, Fall 1986

Paperback sourcebooks in
The Jossey-Bass Higher Education Series

Jossey-Bass Inc., Publishers
San Francisco • London

George H. Voegel (ed.).
Advances in Instructional Technology.
New Directions for Community Colleges, no. 55.
Volume XIV, number 3.
San Francisco: Jossey-Bass, 1986.

New Directions for Community Colleges
Arthur M. Cohen, *Editor-in-Chief;* Florence B. Brawer, *Associate Editor*

New Directions for Community Colleges (publication number USPS 121-710) is published quarterly by Jossey-Bass Inc., Publishers, in association with the ERIC Clearinghouse for Junior Colleges. *New Directions* is numbered sequentially—please order extra copies by sequential number. The volume and issue numbers above are included for the convenience of libraries. Second class postage paid at San Francisco, California, and at additional mailing offices. POSTMASTER: Send address changes to Jossey-Bass Inc., Publishers, 433 California Street, San Francisco, California 94104.

The material in this publication was prepared pursuant to a contract with the Office of Educational Research and Improvement, U.S. Department of Education. Contractors undertaking such projects under government sponsorship are encouraged to express freely their judgment in professional and technical matters. Prior to publication, the manuscript was submitted to the Center for the Study of Community Colleges for critical review and determination of professional competence. This publication has met such standards. Points of view or opinions, however, do not necessarily represent the official view or opinions of the Center for the Study of Community Colleges or the Office of Educational Research and Improvement.

Editorial correspondence should be sent to the Editor-in-Chief, Arthur M. Cohen, at the ERIC Clearinghouse for Junior Colleges, University of California, Los Angeles, California 90024.

Library of Congress Catalog Card Number 85-644753

International Standard Serial Number ISSN 0194-3081

International Standard Book Number ISBN 1-55542-980-7

Cover art by WILLI BAUM

Manufactured in the United States of America

Office of Educational
Research and Improvement
U.S. Department of Education

Ordering Information

The paperback sourcebooks listed below are published quarterly and can be ordered either by subscription or single-copy.

Subscriptions cost $40.00 per year for institutions, agencies, and libraries. Individuals can subscribe at the special rate of $30.00 per year *if payment is by personal check*. (Note that the full rate of $40.00 applies if payment is by institutional check, even if the subscription is designated for an individual.) Standing orders are accepted.

Single copies are available at $9.95 when payment accompanies order, and *all single-copy orders under $25.00 must include payment*. (California, New Jersey, New York, and Washington, D.C., residents please include appropriate sales tax.) For billed orders, cost per copy is $9.95 plus postage and handling. (Prices subject to change without notice.)

Bulk orders (ten or more copies) of any individual sourcebook are available at the following discounted prices: 10-49 copies, $8.95 each; 50-100 copies, $7.96 each; over 100 copies, *inquire*. Sales tax and postage and handling charges apply as for single copy orders.

Please note that these prices are for the academic year 1986-1987 and are subject to change without prior notice. Also, some titles may be out of print and therefore not available for use.

To ensure correct and prompt delivery, all orders must give either the *name of an individual* or an *official purchase order number*. Please submit your order as follows:

Subscriptions: specify series and year subscription is to begin.
Single Copies: specify sourcebook code (such as, CC1) and first two words of title.

Mail orders for United States and Possessions, Latin America, Canada, Japan, Australia, and New Zealand to:
    Jossey-Bass Inc., Publishers
    433 California Street
    San Francisco, California 94104

Mail orders for all other parts of the world to:
    Jossey-Bass Limited
    28 Banner Street
    London EC1Y 8QE

New Directions for Community Colleges Series
Arthur M. Cohen, *Editor-in-Chief*
Florence B. Brawer, *Associate Editor*

CC1   *Toward a Professional Faculty*, Arthur M. Cohen
CC2   *Meeting the Financial Crisis*, John Lombardi
CC3   *Understanding Diverse Students*, Dorothy M. Knoell

CC4	*Updating Occupational Education,* Norman C. Harris
CC5	*Implementing Innovative Instruction,* Roger H. Garrison
CC6	*Coordinating State Systems,* Edmund J. Gleazer, Jr., Roger Yarrington
CC7	*From Class to Mass Learning,* William M. Birenbaum
CC8	*Humanizing Student Services,* Clyde E. Blocker
CC9	*Using Instructional Technology,* George H. Voegel
CC10	*Reforming College Governance,* Richard C. Richardson, Jr.
CC11	*Adjusting to Collective Bargaining,* Richard J. Ernst
CC12	*Merging the Humanities,* Leslie Koltai
CC13	*Changing Managerial Perspectives,* Barry Heermann
CC14	*Reaching Out Through Community Service,* Hope M. Holcomb
CC15	*Enhancing Trustee Effectiveness,* Victoria Dziuba, William Meardy
CC16	*Easing the Transition from Schooling to Work,* Harry F. Silberman, Mark B. Ginsburg
CC17	*Changing Instructional Strategies,* James O. Hammons
CC18	*Assessing Student Academic and Social Progress,* Leonard L. Baird
CC19	*Developing Staff Potential,* Terry O'Banion
CC20	*Improving Relations with the Public,* Louis W. Bender, Benjamin R. Wygal
CC21	*Implementing Community-Based Education,* Ervin L. Harlacher, James F. Gollattscheck
CC22	*Coping with Reduced Resources,* Richard L. Alfred
CC23	*Balancing State and Local Control,* Searle F. Charles
CC24	*Responding to New Missions,* Myron A. Marty
CC25	*Shaping the Curriculum,* Arthur M. Cohen
CC26	*Advancing International Education,* Maxwell C. King, Robert L. Breuder
CC27	*Serving New Populations,* Patricia Ann Walsh
CC28	*Managing in a New Era,* Robert E. Lahti
CC29	*Serving Lifelong Learners,* Barry Heermann, Cheryl Coppeck Enders, Elizabeth Wine
CC30	*Using Part-Time Faculty Effectively,* Michael H. Parsons
CC31	*Teaching the Sciences,* Florence B. Brawer
CC32	*Questioning the Community College Role,* George B. Vaughan
CC33	*Occupational Education Today,* Kathleen F. Arns
CC34	*Women in Community Colleges,* Judith S. Eaton
CC35	*Improving Decision Making,* Mantha Mehallis
CC36	*Marketing the Program,* William A. Keim, Marybelle C. Keim
CC37	*Organization Development: Change Strategies,* James Hammons
CC38	*Institutional Impacts on Campus, Community, and Business Constituencies,* Richard L. Alfred
CC39	*Improving Articulation and Transfer Relationships,* Frederick C. Kintzer
CC40	*General Education in Two-Year Colleges,* B. Lamar Johnson
CC41	*Evaluating Faculty and Staff,* Al Smith
CC42	*Advancing the Liberal Arts,* Stanley F. Turesky
CC43	*Counseling: A Crucial Function for the 1980s,* Alice S. Thurston, William A. Robbins
CC44	*Strategic Management in the Community College,* Gunder A. Myran
CC45	*Designing Programs for Community Groups,* S. V. Martorana, William E. Piland
CC46	*Emerging Roles for Community College Leaders,* Richard L. Alfred, Paul A. Elsner, R. Jan LeCroy, Nancy Armes
CC47	*Microcomputer Applications in Administration and Instruction,* Donald A. Dellow, Lawrence H. Poole

CC48 *Customized Job Training for Business and Industry,* Robert J. Kopecek, Robert G. Clarke
CC49 *Ensuring Effective Governance,* William L. Deegan, James F. Gollattscheck
CC50 *Strengthening Financial Management,* Dale F. Campbell
CC51 *Active Trusteeship for a Changing Era,* Gary Frank Petty
CC52 *Maintaining Institutional Integrity,* Donald E. Puyear, George B. Vaughan
CC53 *Controversies and Decision Making in Difficult Economic Times,* Billie Wright Dziech
CC54 *The Community College and Its Critics,* L. Stephen Zwerling

Contents

Editor's Notes 1
George H. Voegel

1. **Telecourses: Using Technology to Serve Distant Learners** 3
Leslie N. Purdy
Telecourses challenge faculty and administrators to produce quality materials that exploit the special features of television and to design new support services for students who can profit from this new form of instruction.

2. **Satellites Stop Beeping and Start Teaching** 13
Peter Vander Haeghen
Improved broadcast technology and increased use of satellites make it possible for educators to reach previously unserved populations.

3. **Change Through Cooperation: The NILRC Model** 21
Jack A. Weiss, Ralph G. Steinke
Regional cooperative efforts among learning resource centers at different colleges yield many benefits, including cost savings, resource sharing, and coordinated staff development.

4. **Access with Excellence** 29
John E. Roueche, George A. Baker III, Suanne D. Roueche
While the majority of teachers and administrators at American colleges have been grappling with student literacy problems for a long time, they now have at their disposal a vast array of technological possibilities for the effort to improve student persistence and achievement.

5. **Copyrights Revisited** 41
George H. Voegel
The issue of copyright poses serious questions in the area of educational media, particularly for those who produce or copy nonprint media.

6. **Educational Technology in Multicampus Community Colleges: A Decade of Change** 49
Gloria Terwilliger
A recent survey demonstrates that the new and old can coexist successfully within the framework of educational technology as coordinated by the systems and structure of the learning resource center.

**7. Limited Edition: Small Community Colleges Adapt to
New Technologies**   59
Carl D. Cottingham

Small community colleges are ready to take full advantage of advanced instructional technologies. Declining prices and the cost savings of cooperative purchasing will help.

8. Technology for Education: Promises and Problems   65
Kamala Anandam

Despite the application of technology, classroom instruction has changed very little, and while accountability in terms of contact time remains intact, little progress is likely to be made in enhancing the human aspects of teaching.

9. Instructional Technology Mix: Some Considerations   73
George H. Voegel

We must engage in widespread and intensive discussions of the appropriate technological and human mix if we are effectively to serve the needs of community college students.

**10. Sources and Information: Instructional Technology at
Community Colleges**   83
Jim Palmer

Additional materials from the Educational Resources Information Center (ERIC) can be consulted for further information on educational technology at the community college.

Index   95

Editor's Notes

Community colleges are still in the forefront on the use of technology for instruction. From the implementation of comprehensive learning resource centers (LRCs) that embraced a wide range of technology in the 1970s to the adoption in today's LRCs of such new technologies as telecourses and microcomputers, community colleges have to be able to adjust their finite resources in order to provide students with access to these instructional technologies. The purpose of this volume is to provide the reader with some perspective on the adjustments made to the use of technology in instruction since the mid 1970s.

Administrators should be able to find a range of ideas on the changes that technology has wrought in instruction, and they should also be able to take a reflective look through the information presented in several chapters about the rise and fall in the use of some specific equipment and software. Administrators should also be pleased to read about the beneficial effects of consortiums or cooperative membership on the cost of purchasing or leasing a variety of instructional materials now being used. Faculty should take heart from examples provided here which show that community colleges are still being flexible in their support of instructional technology for use in teaching. Such flexibility, in spite of the fact that resources are more limited now than they were a decade ago, is represented by the demonstrated ability of LRCs to change media formats (for example, film has given way to video), drop old technologies, and cautiously implement new technologies. Those concerned primarily with students and their learning will discover that many chapters display a very strong regard for the human qualitites of learners in the context of the application or use of instructional technology.

Some contributors discuss various aspects of the state of the art of the continuing evolution of the use of technology for teaching and learning. These authors give special attention to particulars within the wide range of the application of such technologies. Other authors draw the learner into their discussions by sharing concerns about the background level of the students involved. Cooperative approaches are the subject of one chapter and they are mentioned in a number of other chapters. Copyright issues are also examined. How large and small colleges are coping with technological change is described in some detail, and reflections on the implementation of technology are offered for consideration by the readers. The information, ideas, and suggestions presented in this volume on the use of instructional technology should help community college educators to improve their understanding of the ways in which instructional technology can contribute to effective instruction and set new directions for the teaching-learning process.

George H. Voegel
Editor

George H. Voegel is dean of educational services at William Rainey Harper College in Palatine, Illinios. His responsibilities include a comprehensive learning resource service, adult education, tutoring, and academic computing services. His wide experience with instructional improvement programs, consortium work, and workshops on the appropriate use of technology in instruction and his service to numerous state and national organizations enable him to provide leadership to the community college field on the application of technology to the learning process.

Telecourses challenge faculty and administrators to produce quality materials that exploit the special features of television and to design new support services for students who can profit from this new form of instruction.

Telecourses: Using Technology to Serve Distant Learners

Leslie N. Purdy

Instructional television courses for adult learners are part of a movement in higher education to offer alternative forms of education in order to expand adult access to educational opportunities. The movement began in the nineteenth century with extension and other programs that made it possible for adults to study and receive credit for courses without having to participate in regular, on-campus classroom activities. One form of this alternative learning was correspondence courses, and they remain an established method for taking courses from universities in the United States and Europe. Now distance education comes in many forms. Instructional television courses, often called *telecourses,* are especially prominent.

Telecourses have been created in response to changes in the student population and to the need for lifelong learning. As the number of people wanting some form of postsecondary education has increased, enrollment in institutions of higher education has grown. Not only are increasing numbers of high school graduates seeking a college education, but the trend toward lifelong learning—education for adults at all ages—has also increased the demand for higher education, especially in the form of distance learning. Whether the motives for education are self-enrichment, vocational training or retraining, or a degree, adults are enrolling in all forms of distance learning because they do not have the time, resources, or desire to become full-time students on a campus.

Another factor in the development of new forms of distance education has been the discovery and increasing sophistication of communication technologies. In this century, radio, television, and computers have been added to the printed and spoken word as modes of communication, and educational institutions are exploring ways of utilizing these technologies for purposes of distance learning.

In the United States, examples of distance learning institutions that use television and other new technologies are plentiful. Rio Salado Community College in Arizona and Coastline Community College in California represent nontraditional, two-year colleges established to serve adult distant learners. Dallas County Community College District has been producing and offering high quality telecourses for more than ten years. Empire State College in New York and the LearnAlaska Network of the University of Alaska are four-year institutions that stress distance learning and flexible education programs for adult learners.

Colleges have often cooperated to produce and offer telecourses, and several large consortia now exist for this purpose. Examples of such alliances include the Southern California Consortium for Community College Television, the Bay Area Television Consortium in San Francisco, the Northern Illinois Learning Resources Cooperative based in the Chicago area, and the Eastern Educational Consortium, which covers several northeastern states. Canada has several open learning institutions, such as the ACCESS Consortium in Saskatchewan and the Knowledge Network in British Columbia. The American Association of Community and Junior Colleges has formed the Instructional Telecommunications Consortium to serve as a research and information-sharing agency for schools that offer telecourses. In recognizing the exploding interest in distance and media-based learning, another important national organization, the American Association of Higher Education, publishes a newsletter entitled *Telescan: The Digest of the Center for Learning and Telecommunications*, which reports on articles, books, and speeches on educational uses of telecommunications.

But, while the use of telecourses has become common in the United States and in distance learning institutions throughout the world, criticisms of this form of higher education have been expressed. For many, especially college faculty members, the greatest problem with telecourse instruction is that it tends to separate the teacher from students and students from other students, thus impersonalizing the educational process. Not only does the lack of human interaction offend believers in the traditional pattern whereby a teacher personally delivers instruction, but critics feel that it also threatens faculty control of the curriculum and instructional processes. Telecourses, as used in the United States, are often produced at one institution and then acquired and offered by other educational institutions. Thus, both the technology and the delivery mechanisms appear to bypass local instructors.

Surveys of telecourse students reveal another perspective on this form of instruction. Students praise telecourses because they provide greater flexibility than do campus-based classroom courses. Part-time students can take one or two courses at a time, view programs and study at home, and have some independence in learning whatever seems useful and interesting to them. For these students, classroom instruction is perceived as a closed system that is heavily dominated by individual instructors' points of view and styles of instruction. The opportunity for student autonomy, even anonymity, that telecourses offer is especially appealing to adult students who may feel uncomfortable in a classroom with younger students, who are seemingly more willing to accept the instructor's point of view and teaching styles (Feasley, 1983).

Which view of telecourses is accurate? In order to answer this question, we need to understand the intent of telecourse producers and designers and the assumptions that they have made about the students who take the courses. We also need to consider what if any difference the technology of television makes in the teaching and learning process. This chapter addresses these topics.

Some Theories of Learning Relevant to Distance Education

Producers of distance learning education base their work on a number of educational theories rather than on any one philosophy. These theoretical positions have not always been well articulated by distance learning practitioners, who are often preoccupied with the day-to-day problems of implementation and management.

In general, distance education and telecourses have been built on an individualist theory of knowledge and education. "According to the traditional, Cartesian theory of knowledge, a person can quite effectively learn alone. All we really need in order to learn is a source—a teaching instrument—which may be a book, a television screen, or nature itself" (Bruffee, 1982). According to this perspective, education requires a communication process, but communication does not always need to take the form of discussion with other people. While social relations, such as those involved in discussions, are often useful, they are not essential to learning.

When this theory is applied to televised instruction, it suggests that "Televised programs, both educational and commercial, are designed to convey knowledge in much the same way as a lecture conveys it. Television is a source. As a teaching instrument, it transfers information from the television screen to the mind of the individual viewer" (Bruffee, 1982, p. 27). One implication of this individualist theory of learning is that it expands the possible sources of learning. For adult learners, this seems especially significant, since adults tend to learn from many sources throughout their lives. It also directs study about the learning process to the individual learner instead of restricting it to the teacher.

Developments in psychological research and learning theory have also encouraged educators to consider the individual involved in the learning process. One observer has summarized the impact of this change of focus: "Although the class is the model for education in most schools, there is increasing emphasis on the centrality of the individual learner. The old single-stage model of learning . . . has been abandoned [for] the multistage model with the idea of an individual, idiosyncratic coding or mediation between the stimulus and response . . . The multistage mediational learning concept exposes the delusion that learning is an event of social interaction (Holmberg, 1981, p. 34).

The focus on the individual in the learning process has been an especially productive direction for research on how adults learn, since higher education usually deals with complex types of learning. Often called *cognitive psychology* or *information-processing theory*, this area of psychology has been concerned with "the existing cognitive structures that individuals bring to the learning situation" as well as with the nature of the subject being taught (Wildman and Burton, 1981). Thus, the assumption can be made that, when learning occurs, it is a result of information's being designed and presented in a way appropriate to the learner's cognitive framework. There is no bias toward the delivery of instruction by teachers in classrooms or toward any other single instructional format. Rather, the focus is on the correct design and preparation of the instructional materials and accurate identification of the learning characteristics of the learners, two central precepts in the development of distance learning materials.

Telecourses and distance learning are also indebted to another psychological school of thought, B. F. Skinner's behaviorism. From behaviorism come some of the techniques that have been used in the design of telecourses. Often referred to as the *systems approach*, these techniques have attempted to make instructional design more orderly and scientific by combining what is known about students, the teaching capabilities of the medium, and the structure of the subject matter to produce effective multimedia courses. It is important to note that application of the techniques of the systems approach to the production of distance learning materials does not indicate adoption or acceptance of Skinner's stimulus-response model of learning. Nevertheless, the techniques themselves have proved to be useful and effective both to students and to producers of telecourses.

The two systems approach techniques used in many telecourses are identification of the target group and organization of the course around specific instructional objectives stated in terms of demonstrable student performance (Purdy, 1983). Description of a target group involves studying such things as students' educational background, their motives for taking telecourses in general and a specific course in particular, their age, sex, and family and employment situations. With this information, course developers can choose appropriate teaching strategies and formulate content that is at the students' learning level. Specifying instructional objectives has several advantages. First, objectives help to provide a focus for the lengthy and complex task of producing television courses. A statement of course goals and instructional objectives also provides a vehicle for the organization of course content as well as an objective system for evaluating the effectiveness of a telecourse in reaching its goals. Finally, when given to learners, instructional objectives can help to direct attention, study, and review throughout the course. Regarding the use of objectives, Holmberg (1981, p. 38) observes that "it is natural to regard demonstrable behaviour not as the total effect of learning but as a sign indicating the probability that the desired learning has or has not, taken place." The practices of identifying target audiences and specifying student learning objectives are being adopted in all forms of education, not just in telecourses. Even if these practices do not guarantee good instruction, they provide a means for identifying weak and ineffective instruction.

In summary, the theoretical origins of telecourses are to be found in several disciplines and schools of thought. Yet, they provide the concepts that are central to this form of instruction. Holmberg (1981, p. 38) concludes that, "While . . . the behaviourist school has exerted a strong influence on the practice of distance education, principles emphasized in cognitive learning theory as well as principles from motivation and personality theories and social psychology are evidently decisive for much of what is achieved in this type of education."

The Role of Various Media in Telecourses

If looking at theories of learning helps us to understand more about the learner's side of the learning process, then it is equally important for us to look at the other side, the "source," or, in the case of telecourses, the media used to present the course information. Here, too, there are some basic theories or assumptions about the teaching capabilities of the various media used. Telecourses are not only innovative because they are a form of distance education but because they utilize new communication technologies.

When we study telecourses, it is easy for us to forget that television is but one of several media used to deliver content. In addition to television programs, most telecourses use print media in the form of textbooks and study guides and instructor interaction in the form of correspondence and telephone or face-to-face discussions. Other media can include audiotapes, computers, and newpapers. Of these, the print materials, especially the textbook, carry the bulk of the content of the course. Most telecourses used in American higher education utilize commercially available textbooks that are respected by faculty members for classroom instruction and that have received high marks from students for readability and interest. It is generally accepted that the print medium can present some kinds of information, such as detailed and complex explanations, lists of facts, complex graphic displays, and routine drill and practice, much better than other media can (ITV Center, 1978).

The role and strengths of the print medium for the presentation of information are well understood and accepted. But, while the textbook is an important part of telecourses, it is not the whole course. "A textbook gives all relevant facts, and if it is a good textbook, it does so in a clear and logical way, but it does not guide or teach. That is to say, it does not induce the student to learn . . . A distance-study course guides and teaches by giving complete explanations with elucidating examples, by providing exercises of various kinds, and by constantly referring to what the student has already learned to master" (Holmberg, 1981, p. 56).

The functions of the whole course identified by Holmberg are accomplished in a telecourse by the study guide, the television programs, and the instructor. Thus, it is important to understand that telecourses, as multimedia systems of instruction, are designed so that each of the media used handles specific instructional activities. Further, the media are designed to be coordinated and integrated so that each medium (or component) reinforces the information presented in another component. For example, in one lesson in a course on child psychology ("The Growing Years," 1982, Lesson 13, "Preschool Mental Development"), the textbook may present in some detail the experiments and reasoning that led psychologist Jean Piaget to his theory of conservation as an aspect of cognitive development. The accompanying television program shows reenactments of these famous experiments that vividly demonstrate the theory and show how children of different ages have quite different mental abilities regarding conservation tasks. The study guide provides learning activities and self-test questions to help students ascertain whether they understand and can apply the concepts. And finally the telecourse instructor answers students' questions, suggests and monitors other learning activities, such as direct observation of children, and evaluates student work. Thus, a telecourse is truly a multimedia coordinated instructional package.

The role of the television programs in a telecourse and their effect on learning are the object both of agreement and of debate. On the one hand, "both radio and television, audio and video recordings are usually held to be good motivating forces and assumed to exert greater affective influence than print or written communications" (Holmberg, 1981, p. 65). Most distance educators cite television's potential for demonstration, for bringing unique visuals from laboratories, historical settings, dramatizations, and foreign places as enrichment to the educational process. Some recent research suggests that the television programs have other functions. A University of Mid-America (UMA) study (Brown, 1975, pp. 54-55) reported that "learners in UMA courses [tend] to react negatively to those aspects of the television programs perceived by learners as having exclusively an entertainment function rather than one of instruction." It may be that students watching television for instruction use levels of attention and criteria of quality that differ from those they use when watching television for relaxation and entertainment. The same study concluded that the broadcast television programs serve as a pacing device for students taking the telecourses.

On the other hand, there is also much debate between knowledgeable observers over the specific role of television in learning. We are all familiar with McLuhan's assertion that the medium is the message, which suggests that each medium in some way transforms the content being conveyed. Recent research elaborates on that thesis. For example, Salomon (1979) has presented an extensive analysis of how television utilizes various symbol systems differently than other media. He concludes that a learner will receive different content and different meaning from different symbol systems and that we need to teach people to learn the mental skills necessary for understanding the symbol systems of different media. A similar idea supports various efforts at teaching visual literacy to children at young ages. Yet, others in the field of educational media disagree and assert that media are mere vehicles for presentation of knowledge, not agents that somehow change the knowledge. For example, Clark (1982, p. 60) states that "We cannot validly claim any advantage of one medium over another when student achievement is the issue." Thus, for Clark, the choice of media to be used in a course is determined by convenience, resources, and availability. Both sides agree that television can teach, but they disagree over whether television—indeed, any of the new communication technologies—changes the teaching-learning process in perhaps subtle but pervasive ways. More research is needed to explore the nature of television as an instructional device and the ways in which adult learners react to and learn from television.

Telecourses: Learning from a Distance

Exploring the nature of telecourses means looking at the learners, the media, and finally, the basic method of their operation whereby students are independent and autonomous during much of their course work. What is the effect of distance on students and learning? The answer is probably that while distance between the student and the teacher and other resources of the institution is important, it does not necessarily prevent student learning. The fact that telecourses are designed to appeal to and serve mature and self-motivated learners has already been mentioned. In support of this approach, telecourse producers point to one of the goals of higher education: to promote the growth of student autonomy that leads ultimately to self-directed learning.

For some, the most important aspect of telecourses is in promoting and serving student independence: "The distant student is placed in a situation where he has much greater chances of individually selecting what he is to apply himself to than those conventional students for whom classroom attendance is compulsory" (Holmberg, 1981, p. 26). One result of this freedom is that students may complete only part of the course that is immediately useful and important to them. In light of this learner autonomy and freedom, dropout rates that are higher than those for classroom courses are neither surprising nor undesirable and in Holmberg's view (1981, pp. 19-20), the higher dropout rate "is wholly acceptable and should not be considered a negative comment *provided* students are offered proper facilities. Whether or not they make use of what is offered is up to the individual students."

Yet, however desirable the goal of the student autonomy and self-directed learning may be, the practical reality is that not all telecourse students are ready to profit from the autonomy offered in telecourse instruction. For the less mature student, telecourses may substitute the authority of a television program and a text for the authority of a professor in a classroom. Rather than actively responding to the visual presentation of content, they may passively accept it as a "canned" lecture. And, high dropout rates may be in part the result of immature students who cannot handle the autonomy, a finding reported in research on younger British Open University students (Waters, 1983). Thus, challenging students to think and reason, to respond actively and critically to the course, is a problem for telecourse instruction. And, institutions offering telecourses must identify students for whom distance learning is inappropriate and either help them to learn new study techniques or direct them to other, more supportive instructional situations.

Under the distance learning framework of telecourses, responsibility for learning is placed primarily on the shoulders of the students. However, the responsibility for encouraging learning still rests with faculty and educational institutions. The design, production, acquisition, and offering of the telecourses sets new kinds of responsibilities for all persons involved. First, the components of a telecourse need to be clear, interesting, and flexible. At the same time, they must observe academic standards of accuracy, objectivity, and completeness. A telecourse does not have the classroom's captive audience, and it must show the importance, excitement, and relevance of the subject to the student early in the course if it is to retain that student's voluntary commitment. Further, the institution that offers telecourses needs to design and offer appropriate support services for students who need help in order to profit from and complete the course. Practical considerations, such as enrollment by mail, evening and weekend faculty office hours, telephone office hours, frequent written communication between instructors and students, library use, and purchase of textbooks by mail, as well as prompt feedback to students concerning results of tests and assignments, are but a few of the support services that institutions have offered to telecourse students.

Telecourses are multimedia presentations, not merely a series of television programs, print materials, or correspondence exercises. If telecourses fail to achieve the highest goals of our institutions of higher education, the blame cannot be placed on technology or on the fact of distance between learner and teacher per se. The test of the quality of the learning still rests on all the experience that we offer to students and on what we ask them to do as a result of their learning.

For example, if personal interaction between students and scholars is established as an important part of the educational process, those interactions can be provided even in distance learning situations. If student demonstration of higher-level thinking is a goal, institutions must establish ways of teaching and testing for such skills. Television, telecourses, and distance learning do not inherently prohibit or make impossible the achievement of such experience and goals.

Telecourses use one of the new communications technologies to accomplish distance learning for adults. In doing so, they raise important goals of independence and autonomy for students. They also challenge faculty and administrators to produce quality materials that utilize the qualities of the medium and to provide new kinds of support services for students who like and can profit from this new form of instruction.

References

Brown, L. A. *Learner Responses to the Use of Television in UMA Courses.* Working Paper No. 8. Lincoln, Neb.: University of Mid-America, 1975.

Bruffee, K. A. "CLTV: Collaborative Learning Television." *Educational Communications and Technology Journal,* 1982, *30,* 26–40.

Clark, R. E. "Review of Media in Instruction: 60 Years of Research." *Educational Communications and Technology Journal,* 1982, *30,* 60.

Feasley, C. E. *Serving Learners at a Distance: A Guide to Program Practices.* ASHE-ERIC Higher Education Research Report No. 5. Washington, D.C.: Association for the Study of Higher Education, 1983.

Holmberg, B. *Status and Trends of Distance Education.* New York: Nichols, 1981.

ITV Center. *ITV Close-up: The First Six Years.* Dallas: Dallas County Community College District, 1978.

Purdy, L. "The Role of Instructional Design in Telecourses." In L. Purdy (ed.), *Reaching New Students Through New Technologies.* Dubuque, Iowa: Kendall/Hunt, 1983.

Salomon, G. *Interaction of Media, Cognition, and Learning: An Exploration of How Symbolic Forms Cultivate Mental Skills and Affect Knowledge Acquisition.* San Francisco: Jossey-Bass, 1979.

"The Growing Years." Telecourse produced by The Coast Community Colleges, the University of California at San Diego, and McGraw-Hill, 1982.

Waters, G. "Learning from the Open University: The Limits of Telecommunications." In L. Purdy (ed.), *Reaching New Students Through New Technologies,* Dubuque, Iowa: Kendall/Hunt, 1983.

Wildman, T. M., and Burton, J. K. "Integrating Learning Theory with Instructional Design." *Journal of Instructional Development,* 1981, *4,* 5-14.

Leslie N. Purdy is director of telecourse development and production at Coastline Community College in Costa Mesa, California.

Improved broadcast technology and increased use of satellites make it possible for educators to reach previously unserved populations.

Satellites Stop Beeping and Start Teaching

Peter Vander Haeghen

Distance learning in higher education reaches students who cannot or do not want to come to college campuses. Often their experiences with distance learning later bring them to the campus to complete their educational goals, goals that they had felt were unattainable. A new attempt at reaching more of these potential students by increasing curriculum selection is now being developed by the Telecourse People and the Instructional Telecommunications Consortium of the American Association of Community and Junior Colleges (AACJC).

Many distance learning students need college credit for their degree goals. Current statistics indicate that a majority of telecourse students are degree oriented. But, there is a very large number of adults who are interested only in the information, not in the credit, offered by telecourses and related series. Some research by both the Public Broadcasting System (PBS) and Coast Telecourses came up with similar numbers in research projects that were conducted several years apart. This research indicates that there may be as many as 250 educational viewers for every enrolled student. As many continuing education program directors know, these unenrolled "students" need and want information. And, they are willing to pay for it, as the PBS stations that ran TV Ontario's computer literacy series "Bits and Bytes" quickly found out when more than 35,000 people each sent $70 to those stations as part of a non-college-based learning experience. The only college participation came from a few colleges that offered the course for college credit aside from, not as part of, the **PBS Computer Academy**.

More and more people are turning to television for information as well as for entertainment. Some information resources for these people are PBS, specialty cable channels, bookstores, and home video stores, to which vending machines in grocery stores are soon to be added. So, who cares how the video is delivered, as long as a college issues credit? The time has arrived for a satellite service to allow the college, station, or cable system to use academic programming to serve the distance learner.

Satellite Telecourse Survey

In January 1985, a questionnaire was sent to more than 300 telecourse customers in the United States. The purpose of the survey was to find out whether telecourse users would be interested in a satellite channel completely dedicated to the offering of credit college courses that could distribute telecourses through any available local broadcast delivery system. The cost of the service was estimated to be about $3,000 per college per year, plus individual course leases (at a reduced price). It was assumed that enhanced underwriting statements run between course segments would help to pay for the service.

Of the eighty respondents to this survey, forty-six were two-year public community or vocational colleges, eleven were upper-division institutions, one was a hospital, one was a school district, five were PBS stations, one was a Canadian college, and the nature of ten was unknown. Of the responding community colleges, 84.8 percent said they would support the channel, as compared with 62.5 percent of the upper-division colleges. A large majority of community college respondents were enthusiastically supportive of the concept. Sixty-three percent of these respondents felt that such a service would improve utilization. Fifty-three respondents in all indicated that they would use the service full-time on their cable channel and allow the enhanced underwriting statements to run. In addition to cable, twenty-one schools had access to ITFS (Instructional Television Fixed Services, a 2,500 megahertz band television system), and five had access to low-power transmission stations.

The community colleges responding to the survey represented 31,110 telecourse enrollments annually through 476 course leases. Overall, survey respondents had 73,759 enrollments from 810 leases. General comments ranged from "good luck" to great skepticism, to important suggestions for success. In general, there was a great deal of support for the project from this particular survey group who happened to represent the major telecourse users in the country.

The Hope of Transmission Technology

A long-nurtured goal—using technology to meet the needs of students who are currently unable to attend classes on a college campus—is approaching realization. The means is the delivery of college-level courses to all Americans and people around the world via television and other electronic delivery systems. The major technological hurdle, expensive mass delivery of huge amounts of educational material, is being overcome. Today, the number of satellites and receiving stations across the nation located at broadcast stations, cable systems, colleges, and homes makes this technological delivery of instruction as easy as turning on a television set anywhere in the country.

Satellite dishes are so inexpensive that they are commonly found in the backyards of American family homes. These are not the homes of the rich or even of the upper middle class. These are farm homes, homes in small towns and large cities, even condominiums. There are so many satellites in the communication ring of space above this nation that a real parking problem is beginning to develop. No longer is satellite communication to the home something from science fiction. It is now as commonplace as the television sets we watch. It is the pivot point for delivery of most programming viewed on both commercial and public television, whether open or closed broadcast.

So, where has higher education been in this technology? PBS has made major headway in delivery of college-level programs to stations and colleges. The Learning Channel has also provided an excellent resource of quality college telecourses through cable systems. Regional networks, such as Central Education Network (CEN) and Southern Educational Communications Association (SECA), are actively involved in the delivery of higher education programming, often via satellite. However, they all have one thing in common: The educational programming that they deliver is only part of a larger program service for other educational or entertainment audiences. Even the specialized satellite teleconference networks do not deliver a full-time higher educational programming service. Such systems as the National University Teleconference Network (NUTN) have met a specific need for college and universities by providing teleconferences that bring current topics and personalities to students all over the country—live and in some cases interactively. The market void or need is for a full-time higher education telecourse service that provides basic two- or three-credit-hour college-level courses.

There are several reasons why a telecourse channel has not yet been started. Most of these reasons center on the financial problems associated with the operation of such a service. The other problems include a lack of sufficient programming, a lack of satellite access or the money needed to buy it, a lack of the promotional expertise needed to sell the service, and a lack of institutional support from enough community colleges and universities around the country to make it possible. Still other reasons involve problems with the techniques of delivery, lack of focus on customer service, and the question of the academic credibility of distance learning courses or instruction through television.

Except in a few rare cases, community colleges have not climbed on the electronic distance learning bandwagon. This may be due in part to the basically conservative nature of their business. The rhetoric about low-quality instruction and loss of teaching positions that this form of technology often elicits has not been justified. Even though teachers fear that this technology will lower academic standards and take away teaching jobs, research over many years has shown both that this is a valid instructional delivery system and that it does not eliminate jobs.

A new development in the use of technological delivery of higher education to students is forming outside the academic system in an area least expected—private industry. With the advent of true satellite broadcast delivery directly to the home, at least one commercial broadcasting company is considering the delivery of credit and noncredit college courses to homes on a $300 24-inch home satellite dish. The dish will receive a variety of entertainment and educational channels. There will be no monthly fee, and no special equipment is needed beyond the dish. This company is seriously conducting extensive market research into the possibility of delivering college-level education for profit.

The concept is not all that unusual when compared with the private colleges or proprietary technical schools that have correspondence schools and training centers all over the country. They have been educationally and financially successful, even though their offerings have often been criticized by the academic institutions. It must be admitted that they know how to analyze the marketplace, provide a needed service, and make a profit at it. To make that profit, these organizations have eliminated many of the sacred cows of academia, such as number of hours of teaching load (instructors work a forty-hour week), tenure (instructors perform at an acceptable level, or they are no longer in the employ of the school), and the publish-or-perish syndrome (instructors are there to teach). In addition, instructors work all year around without benefit of summers off, Christmas and Easter or spring breaks, and semester breaks. In other words, these schools are in the learning business. To maintain such a business, they must produce a quality product. At the same time, they must not price themselves out of the market, or the clients will no longer come to them, just as in any other business. The signs are clear: Community colleges and four-year universities have an opportunity to provide leadership in the technological delivery of instruction for higher education.

If they ignore this opportunity, they may lose potential students to more responsive providers of educational services.

The Adult Learning Service (ALS) of the PBS has made a gallant effort to expand access to electronic learning systems (telecourses in this case). However, it had some unfortunate start-up problems with many of the colleges that were served. ALS has exclusive rights to broadcast distribution of Annenberg Foundation-funded courses, which promises to provide many new and well-produced educational series for many years. The ALS is taking steps to improve overall service to participating colleges, and it will continue to be a key provider of excellent educational programming. The major drawback of the PBS Adult Learning Service, from the perspective of colleges, has been the requirement to use only the PBS station or to get a written waiver from the station in order to use another delivery system. Local stations rightfully want and need exclusivity in their market if they are going to get their share of the revenues. These are valid considerations, but they have had the effect of tying the hands of the colleges.

The Concept of the Telecourse Channel

The Telecourse Channel concept was originated by the Telecourse People consortium in response to a general plea from telecourse users for a more college-oriented delivery service for telecourses. Coastline Community College, through Coast Telecourses, provided impetus for the concept with strong support from the other consortium members. Now, the Instructional Telecommunications Consortium (ITC) of the AACJC has taken over development of the project. With its leadership, the concept promises to hold even greater service potential than it did as originally planned.

The Telecourse Channel would provide college-level courses via satellite to any educational institution that was willing to pay an annual fee of about $3,000 and a small lease fee for each course that it used. The annual fee allows the college to distribute the entire twenty-four-hour-a-day service through its own cable system, ITFS, low-power, or any other delivery available without additional charge. The college pays approximately $400 to $500 per course plus a fee for each student enrolled in credit or noncredit activities. The courses would be leased directly from the producers or distributors. Besides the freedom from restriction on delivery systems and access to as many as forty courses each semester, the college would be able to offer open entry-open exit, short-term, and flexible scheduling. Other services being considered include classroom support materials, in-service, computer software, audio programs, and management information. It will take some time to implement these secondary services.

Under the Telecourse Channel concept, the college would determine its own destiny and maintain control of the educational process. The video portion of the courses would be delivered to meet as many college scheduling concerns as possible. However, the college would determine how to use the video resource. Faculty would be selected and paid for by the college that offered the course. Support systems for the student would be controlled by the college, as is currently done. Credit for the course would also be issued by the local school.

Students have windows of availability—times when they can watch a program. The Telecourse Channel would repeat programs in order both to open windows of availability and to provide opportunities for review. However, it remains the responsibility of the local college to ensure that the quality of the support system meets the expectations of the students. Watching television does not make a comprehensive learning experience. It is the college faculty and support system along with text, study guide, and assignments that make the experience a course.

Unlike attempts of the past to use satellites to establish a national higher education program, the Telecourse Channel project is strictly a telecourse video distribution system aimed at serving colleges through lower-cost telecourses. The channel will help to escalate a delicate program cycle. That cycle begins with the cost of designing and producing a good telecourse—close to $1 million. Production of such courses takes outside investment, which is predicated in part on the prospect of return on investment. High budgets generate good-quality video and design. Good quality means increased use. Increased use means greater financial return for investors. Greater financial return means increased interest by investors, and increased investment means more quality telecourses. Therefore, it is important for the producers to seek greater use of their products so that users have greater selection and larger enrollments.

Such a service will be expensive to operate. Initial estimates for such a service, assuming that producers provide courses to the service for free, are more than $1 million per year. The financing will be the major challenge. In order to raise $1 million a year, some creative financial thought has produced a plan that is currently being pursued. This plan involves a technique called *enhanced underwriting*. The technique is currently being tested by several PBS stations. Enhanced underwriting allows an underwriter to add something to the underwriting statement. Traditional underwriting statements take the form: "This program is brought to you by," followed by the name of the underwriting company. Enhanced underwriting not only acknowledges the underwriter's name but allows the company's logo to be displayed and a statement about the company's products to be added. The PBS guidelines for enhancements are quite specific and clearly define the conditions of use.

The Telecourse Channel would carry the enhanced underwriting concept much further. The Channel is to be operated as a nonprofit organization expressly to provide an educational programming service to colleges and universities, but because the programming will be distributed by local colleges through any means at their disposal, the enhancements can be longer and more explicit. This freedom from restriction would increase the incentives to underwriters to support a telecourse or a block of time. If the underwriter realizes that he can reach a very targeted audience at little expense, compared to the cost of commercial television, the underwriter appreciates that his support has "value returned." That value returned may be increased product awareness, increased corporate awareness, corporate image, or some combination thereof.

Programs or blocks of time would be offered to underwriters on a yearly basis. For example, an underwriter might wish to support a specific program series each time it was distributed. A half-hour segment could cost $95,000 for the year. If the series was repeated, the underwriter might wish to support each repeat for another $95,000. Another possibility is that the underwriter would want to support certain time slots in the day regardless of the programming. Again, the underwriter could do so at a fixed annual rate per year. What does the underwriter get for his support? The underwriter's company gets national exposure to a prescreened audience. This audience is made up of older adults who have families, jobs, motivated educational goals, and purchasing power. The underwriter also gets national recognition as a supporter of education in the United States. And, the underwriter gets thirty seconds before and thirty seconds after each program to make the underwriting statement. The cost of such support is small compared to what most underwriting companies would pay for regular commercial advertising.

The college has the option of running the underwriting statements or not, depending on the agreements that it has with distributors or the regulations that govern its delivery systems. It would be the user's responsibility to remove the enhancements if it does not want them to run. The Telecourse Channel would run the underwriting statements in their entirety. It serves users of the channel best if colleges that can run the underwriting statements do so in order to encourage underwriters to continue their support.

The overall goal of the Telecourse Channel is to increase utilization of telecourses by colleges and universities by increasing access and selection. But, how do you increase telecourse utilization when most colleges can spend only a fixed amount of money on leases? This utilization factor has been a major concern of the system's planning group. One way of increasing utilization is by lowering prices. From the distributor's viewpoint, this creates a serious problem because of fixed overhead. Lowering lease fees on a product that has a slim profit margin can quickly turn black ink to red. High overhead is chiefly due to the percent of return that producers have to give back to investors. Investors are crucial to the development of the product, and their needs must be accommodated.

Assuming that the college budget for telecourse leases is fixed, distributors are gambling that the college will lease more courses because the unit cost has dropped. It is hoped that expanding offerings will spur increased enrollments by telecourse students. Increased enrollment should increase demand, college budgets, and use of courses. It is a long range marketing venture, and a gamble, that the Telecourse People are taking for improved distribution and increased utilization of telecourses in distance learning.

Toward the Future

Public higher education must face the fact that electronic technology is here to stay and that it will have an effect on the lives of us all. Educators who can accept this fact will guide the technology to ensure the most effective utilization and quality. Those who cannot accept it will stand by and watch other agencies take a critical educational process away from them and turn a profit with a product that has been available for years. The Telecourse Channel is an attempt to bring this exciting learning alternative to more colleges and more people inexpensively. Only the people in the academic institutions can answer the question, Will we use and control it, or will we ignore and lose it to other providers?

Peter Vander Haeghen is a faculty member at Coast Community College in Costa Mesa, California.

Regional cooperative efforts among learning resource centers at different colleges yield many benefits, including cost savings, resource sharing, and coordinated staff development.

Change Through Cooperation: The NILRC Model

Jack A. Weiss, Ralph G. Steinke

Community colleges were widely recognized for their comprehensive and innovative programs during a decade of rapid growth in the 1970s. Looking ahead to the 1980s, Breneman and Nelson (1980, p. 73) predicted an "increased tension between mission and finance" and colleges were forced to deal with the realities of leveling enrollments and increasing financial constraints. This prediction has indeed become a very real fact of life for today's community college leaders.

The learning resources center (LRC) has emerged as the common organizational unit for the provision of a wide range of instructional support services. Although LRC programs vary from one college to the next, the model usually includes library technical services, library public services, media production, and audiovisual (AV) equipment maintenance and distribution. Other services found in LRC programs include reprographics (duplication centers), computer labs, learning labs, institutional archives, and telecourse programs. In justifying their programs, LRC professionals often take the position that healthy library and AV services help to improve the quality of instruction. They argue that learning labs and strong tutoring support help to maintain enrollment by keeping high-risk students in classes. However, the bottom line is that these support services are usually money consumers, not money makers. As such, they are vulnerable when colleges face a serious budget situation and are forced to make difficult decisions about maintaining programs.

Bush and Ames (1984, p. 73) have identified technology and human resources development as the two major obstacles that lie ahead for community college leaders. They urge proactive planning as a strategic tool for dealing with these obstacles. Given their unique function in the community colleges, LRC professionals have had broad exposure to technology with a strong services orientation. They are well prepared to provide institutional leadership in addressing technological change and human resources development. Several midwestern community colleges have had more than a decade of successful experience related to these issues, and they have augmented institutional leadership through a learning resources cooperative.

The primary purpose of this chapter is to examine the LRC cooperative as a positive tool for dealing with technological change and human resources development. It will use as a model the Northern Illinois Learning Resources Cooperative (NILRC), and it will highlight benefits in four areas: the cooperative purchase of supplies, equipment, and educational materials; resource sharing; staff development; and information sharing.

The intent in using NILRC as a model for regional cooperatives is to identify some of the factors that have contributed to its success over the past ten years. Specific examples will be given. These success factors can be applied in other settings as colleges face the issues of technological change and human resources development.

The NILRC Background

NILRC was formed in 1973 with the help of an Illinois Community College Board planning grant of $8,000. The grant was awarded through the Higher Education Cooperative Act (HECA) and provided seed money that allowed LRC representatives to begin meeting on a monthly basis. The original emphasis of the members was on the sharing of locally produced instructional materials.

Just as with individuals, organizations have personalities, and NILRC's personality as a new organization was characterized by a spontaneity and openness to new ideas. However, an organization's personality is in large part a composite of the personalities and interests of individual members. From an interest in sharing locally produced instructional materials, the founding members broadened their concerns to such issues as cooperative purchasing, information and resources sharing, and staff development. In fact, all these concerns then became the foundation on which the cooperative was constructed.

As the group's interests widened, it became important from a legal standpoint to obtain the individual and institutional protection afforded by a not-for-profit corporation status. NILRC obtained its charter in May 1975. Since that time, membership in NILRC has grown from eight to thirty-seven institutions. A number of pending applications are being considered.

NILRC Success Factors

A commonly shared community college learning resources philosophy is at the core of NILRC's success. All members believe in comprehensive, integrated learning resources programs that extend to the educational community as well as to the community at large. Such similar thinking produces a climate that is conducive to elevating the concerns of the individual members to an interinstitutional level.

NILRC colleges are located close to the city of Chicago. The practical advantage is one of saving time and money. It is easy for delegates to drive or carpool to monthly board meetings. All fifteen full member colleges are located within a seventy-mile radius of the city of Chicago, and associate membership is extended to institutions outside this area. Member colleges take turns hosting board meetings and other activities. Thus, delegates spend their time more efficiently by meeting, not by traveling.

A significant and certainly most critical reason for NILRC's success has been the human element. The organization was formed at the grassroots operational level by learning resources people. Its structure developed along a bottom-to-top line of communication, not along the more common top-to-bottom model. As a result, its agenda focuses on issues and practical problems experienced by learning resources staff.

The cooperative spirit and trust among NILRC people are best exemplified by the level of information sharing among members. Regular meetings allow delegates from member colleges to know the diverse interests and strengths of other delegates and institutions. Everyone soon knows whom to contact for answers concerning a particular field of expertise. Important developments that may be of interest to NILRC members are reported at the regular meetings or shared informally, when necessary, over the telephone. This practice of information sharing at monthly meetings is often identified by members as one of the most valuable benefits of the organization—one that meets an important individual professional development need. The end result of informal sharing has internally been to build and strengthen the pool of human talent, thereby benefiting all member institutions. Externally, it has thrust NILRC people into active roles in local, regional, state, and national organizations.

The organization's bylaws and membership agreements provide the umbrella of legal protection necessary for dealing with NILRC internal and external affairs, and they establish a unique framework for governance. In addition, they buttress the common community college learning resources concept. The bylaws encourage a rotation of elected officers, thus maximizing the development of leadership qualities among delegates. One effect of shared governance is that over the course of time the large majority of delegates approach matters from a group perspective rather than from the view of a single institution. Moreover, rotation of leadership prevents either an institution or an individual from dominating the activities and decisions of the cooperative. Therefore, NILRC meetings present an open forum in which delegates can discuss and act on the issues freely and candidly.

The bylaws and membership agreements are also characterized by minimum requirements. All that is actually mandated of a full member institution is regular attendance by its delegate at meetings and the payment of the annual dues. Associate members need only to pay dues. Out of such an arrangement comes what can best be termed organizational fluidity. Operational goals are annually formulated, reviewed, and modified. Delegates and member institutions can volunteer and participate in cooperative projects of their own choosing. Each institution is easily able to maintain its autonomy.

The dues structures and voting method make further contributions to cooperative flexibility. Annual dues of $300 per institution were established in 1975, and for full members they have not increased since. This low fee has made it possible for even the smallest colleges with a limited budget to join and enjoy the cost benefits of group contracts. In combination with the one vote per institution stipulated in the bylaws, the dues structure has prevented the development of voting blocs. No large-college-versus-small-college or have-versus-have-not phenomenon has occurred. In fact, membership privileges have equated well with member responsibilities. Smaller colleges, which are often more flexible organizationally than larger schools because of their size, have been able to meet more immediate needs, such as furnishing logistical support services on short notice. The larger institutions frequently have made contributions by sharing special facilities, material, and human resources when the occasion demanded.

The success that has resulted from the factors just outlined has not gone unnoticed, and it has resulted in a degree of emulation. Two other cooperatives have been developed within Illinois along the NILRC model: the Mid-Illinois Learning Resources Cooperative (MILRC) and the Southern Illinois Learning Resources Cooperative (SILRC). They, too, resemble neither a number of regional television consortia that focus only on one specific activity nor certain national consortia that have more dispersed missions or purposes. Like NILRC, they have served their members in a multifaceted manner.

Benefits of NILRC Membership

All of the success factors just enumerated can be regarded as such because of the very real benefits that have resulted from cooperation. Membership benefits originate from cooperative purchasing, information and resources sharing, and staff development.

Cooperative Purchasing. The most evident benefit in terms of cost-effectiveness has occurred in the leasing and purchase of instructional television materials. Consortium pricing has made it possible for even the smallest colleges to acquire materials far beyond their financial means if they acted as individuals. Indeed, the considerable savings realized in the cost of instructional television software, particularly telecourses, has been a significant reason why many institutions have applied for membership in the cooperative.

As television matters generated more activity, they consumed more time as well. Recognizing this, the Telecommunications Advisory Group (TAG) was established as a NILRC standing committee. Formed in April 1981, it consists of telecourse coordinators from the NILRC colleges that are active or interested in discussing educational television matters. Institutional commitments to lease or purchase are made at TAG meetings, and a designated member of the group then negotiates with producers or distributors. The status of television affairs is reported at regular NILRC meetings by the TAG chairperson. In this way, NILRC delegates are kept informed about television developments without the subject's monopolizing a large amount of meeting time.

Added benefits to individual colleges have resulted from the cooperative's membership in a national organization, the Instructional Telecommunications Consortium (ITC), an affiliate of the American Association of Community and Junior Colleges. Composed of producer and user institutions and consortia from the U.S. and Canada, the ITC provides information sharing and production opportunities in which every NILRC college can participate.

Cooperative purchasing agreements extend beyond the instructional television or telecourse area. Group purchases of commercially produced sixteen-millimeter films and videotapes have been successfully negotiated with a number of major producers and distributors, which have made large portions of their holdings available at attractive prices. Other agreements have been consummated with book vendors and audiovisual supply companies. Negotiations are presently in process with library suppliers and computer software vendors.

Information and Resources Sharing. A less tangible but nevertheless equally valuable benefit involves the information and resources exchanged among NILRC members. This sharing can best be exemplified by the research and development of a computerized software package for community college learning resources centers. A team of NILRC personnel composed of librarians, audiovisual specialists, and computer experts developed a plan for the implementation of an automated learning resources package. With the aid of an approximately $200,000 award to the cooperative by the U.S. Department of Education, further research and development as well as initial installation was carried out at Elgin Community College, the host site. The computer package, referred to by the acronym CALS (Comprehensive Automated Learning Resources System), is a flexible LRC management system designed to operate in an IBM computer environment. It accommodates all media formats and satisfies a variety of LRC service needs, including on-line circulation control, audiovisual equipment scheduling, art department slide collection retrieval, and records management. A wide variety of reports are generated, either automatically or on request. Future plans include the development and testing of an on-line catalogue with patron access modules.

Unlike turnkey systems that require the purchase of separate equipment, CALS uses the college's own computer equipment. Data processing staff handle routine maintenance. This conceptual design helps to keep the costs of automation down. The higher degree of integration in CALS also greatly enhances LRC services without requiring additional staff, another cost issue. CALS software is marketed through CALS Services Group, Ltd., a team of community college people with a unique combination of skills and interests in media services, librarianship, and computer technology.

As the cooperative spirit of NILRC people has increased, the level of information sharing among them has risen correspondingly. Formally, the sharing process takes place at regular monthly meetings where delegates are able to draw upon and benefit from the diverse areas of expertise of other delegates. Informally, delegates often share ideas while car pooling to regular board or committee meetings. With increasing frequency, much informal sharing occurs by telephone. The development of the formal telephone network has spawned an annual NILRC activity: publication of the *Illinois Learning Resources Personnel Directory*. The directory contains the names, addresses, and telephone numbers of all Illinois public community colleges and the names, titles, and telephone extensions of their learning resources staff members.

To make information sharing even more efficient, the cooperative currently has under study the development of its own electronic mail system. Such a system would not only be used by learning resources personnel, but it would be offered to other administrators in order to expand cost and time-saving benefits to each college. In addition, it would serve to raise the visibility of learning resources in a positive sense before higher administration.

Staff Development. NILRC has taken an active role in planning growth and development activities for its members in order to prevent professional hardening of the arteries. Tightened budgets, technological changes, and decreased staff turnover due to the economic environment all contribute to the need for a healthy staff development program. Staff development activities usually occur as the result of two processes. The first is an evolutionary one whereby a matter increasingly consumes more time and attention of members. The result is the creation of a subgroup comprised of expert, interested personnel who then concern themselves with the subject. Examples of such groups are the Telecommunications Advisory Group described earlier and an on-line users group made up of library professionals concerned with the accessing of bibliographic data bases.

The second process is more ad hoc by nature in that special topics of interest are focused upon as potential workshop activities. The systematic planning and scheduling of these events is carried out by a NILRC delegate. Examples of past activities include workshops in management techniques for LRC administrators, on-line bibliographic search strategies for reference librarians, microcomputer applications for LRC staff, equipment repair for audiovisual technicians, and demonstration of new equipment for evaluative purposes. Workshops dealing with such emerging technologies as interactive learning systems are in the planning stages.

Conclusion

The NILRC experience conveys an important message to community colleges in general and to learning resources centers in particular. The message is that cooperation can be most advantageous in a climate of stable or declining enrollments and economic constraints on the one hand and of rapid technological change on the other. The dilemma that educators face in such a climate is that they are torn between taking the risks they know changing technology requires and spending funds that they know are limited.

Cooperation is one way by which such a dilemma can be circumvented. As NILRC has demonstrated, colleges are encouraged to take risks because cooperation minimizes the risk. NILRC's success with the delivery of instruction via telecourses is a prime example. Cost savings to each institution permit not only implementation but continued expansion of a nontraditional yet increasingly viable method of education at a time when no additional dollars are available. In short, cooperation gives institutions the leverage they need to innovate.

There is a psychological advantage to cooperation as well. Technological change must be accompanied by an attitudinal change. Instruction and academic support of instruction can only change if the personnel involved can cope and adjust. Cooperation, through the sharing of new ideas and experiences, removes the threat that individuals feel when conditions necessitate change. The support provided by an informational network of fellow professionals has a reciprocal effect of lending increasing strength to the group as well as to the individual.

Finally, truly successful cooperation calls for an exercise in diplomacy and tact. Each cooperative delegate is an autonomous agent of his or her institution, and as such each delegate is on an equal footing with every other delegate. Authority is not a factor among cooperative delegates. Instead, the gentle art of persuasion holds sway. In such an atmosphere, the ultimate in participatory decision making, the real grassroots learning experience, takes place.

What, then, can be learned from the NILRC model? The cooperative is not unique in its balance of the philosophical with the pragmatic, nor in the nature of the individuals and institutions that comprise it, nor in the length of time for which it has existed. Its uniqueness stems from a combination of all these factors with the spirit of voluntarism that prevails among members, for NILRC employs no full-time paid staff. Instead, it demonstrates a record of measurable achievements—the most important of which is the ability to cope with change—that cooperation can bring over the long run when like-minded professionals recognize the need for it and are willing to do something about it.

References

Breneman, D. W., and Nelson, S. C. "The Community College Mission and Patterns of Funding." In G. B. Vaughan (ed.), *Questioning the Community College Role*. New Directions for Community Colleges, no. 32. San Francisco: Jossey-Bass, 1980.

Bush, R. W., and Ames, W. C. "Leadership and Technological Innovation." In R. A. Alfred, P. A. Elsner, R. J. Lecroy, and N. Armes (eds.), *Emerging Roles for Community College Leaders*. New Directions for Community Colleges, no. 46. San Francisco: Jossey-Bass, 1984.

Jack A. Weiss is director of learning resources at Elgin Community College, Elgin, Illinois, and a founding member and past president of the Northern Illinois Learning Resources Cooperative.

Ralph G. Steinke is director of learning resources at Waubonsee Community College, Sugar Grove, Illinois, and current president of the Northern Illinois Learning Resources Cooperative as well as telecourse contracts manager.

While the majority of teachers and administrators at American colleges have been grappling with student literacy problems for a long time, they now have at their disposal a vast array of technological possibilities for improving student persistence and achievement.

Access with Excellence

John E. Roueche, George A. Baker III, Suanne D. Roueche

The nation's colleges and universities are now enrolling freshmen who demonstrate unconscionable deficiencies in reading, writing, figuring, and problem-solving abilities. Many of these institutions can expect that at least one half of their entering students will not be reading above an eighth-grade level, that they will not have been expected or required to write papers of any length or quality, and that they will not have completed math courses traditionally associated with college entrance requirements. The grades of today's high school graduates may suggest high levels of academic ability but the requirements have been so low that a student's grade point average provides an inflated view of the student's real abilities. A recent study by the Educational Testing Service sponsored by the National Center for Education Statistics "claims that the decline in test scores between 1972 and 1980 was caused by decreased academic rigor in the high school curriculum and by a drop in the amount of time students spent on homework" (Hertling, 1984, p. 10). Findings from other studies indicating that no state competency exams require more than a ninth-grade reading level for high school graduation and that many school systems have eliminated some traditional skill requirements—for example, mathematics—altogether for obtaining a diploma provide further cause for concern that the academic skills of high school students will continue to decline (Roueche and others, 1984).

G. H. Voegel (ed.). *Advances in Instructional Technology.*
New Directions for Community Colleges, no. 55. San Francisco: Jossey-Bass, Fall 1986.

In the interests of determining how American colleges and universities were meeting this challenge, we conducted a national survey to determine the extent of the national literacy problem and to identify the common program and service elements that were in place (Roueche and others, 1984). Not surprisingly, we found that a large majority of all colleges and universities—no matter what their size, selectivity, or prestige—were experiencing major literacy problems with entering students. Having verified the dimensions of the literacy problem, we turned to the identification, description, and organization of strategies contributing significantly to a potential solution.

An institution's commitment to provide a viable educational opportunity for any student is reflected in its functional organization of courses and programs that build on student's academic strengths, that instruct for the remediation and development of academic weaknesses, and that collectively lend themselves to the teaching of the content and skills necessary for certification or degree attainment.

From our unique vantage points—the National Institute for Staff and Organizational Development (NISOD) consortium and its *Innovation Abstracts* in particular—we enjoy ongoing formal and informal opportunities to identify and observe in action many innovative, successful strategies for providing the strong instructional framework and the support that the majority of all students demand for success. A recent study of outstanding community colleges has offered us a comprenhesive view of some of the best (Roueche and Baker, 1986). We highlight here some of those strategies—strategies that have proved over time to offer access with excellence by applying the best available information about promoting student academic success to the latest thing in technology. These strategies are being implemented in institutions that recognize the importance of improving their traditional or micro instructional systems—that is, in the systems specific to individual student needs, classrooms, and programs—and incorporating them into a broad, macro instructional system that involves the entire institution and that has at its heart the critical issue of student success. Analyzing the data from our recent national survey provided us with a macro-level model for a low-achiever instructional system (Figure 1) if you will, that capitalizes on the latest efforts towards an instructional system. It has been widely acknowledged by leaders in the field of educational technology that the greatest contribution that technology will make is not in hardware or software but in the application of a systematic approach applying the means (messages, personnel, materials, devices, methods, learning environments, and so forth) to the end of bringing about more effective instruction. Such systematic technology cannot fail to improve instruction and use of technology for all students.

We offer here, in broad brush strokes, a discussion of the responses that appear to have the most potential for providing the strong instructional system framework and the support that the majority of students

Figure 1. Macro Model of a Low-Achiever Instructional System

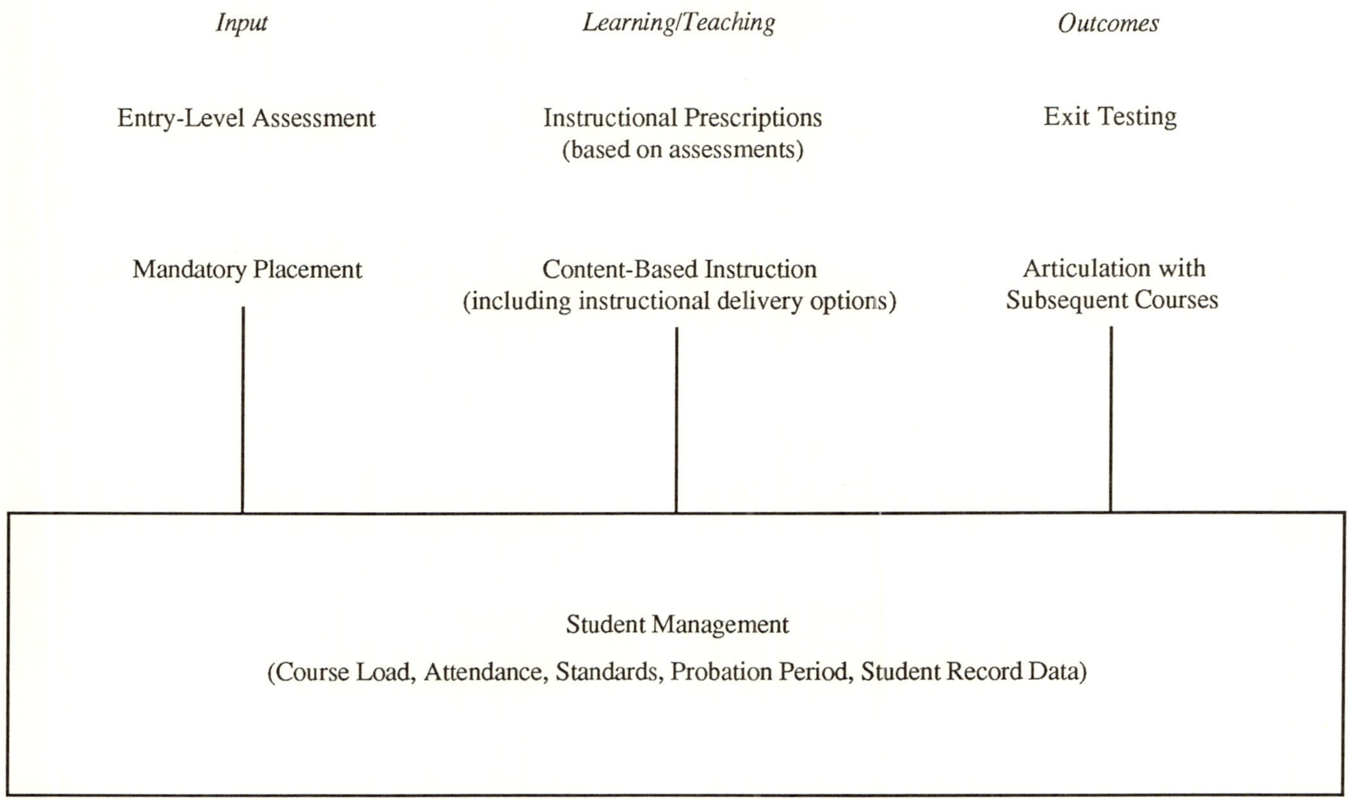

Input	Learning/Teaching	Outcomes
		Exit Testing
		Articulation with Subsequent Courses
Entry-Level Assessment	Instructional Prescriptions (based on assessments)	
	Content-Based Instruction (including instructional delivery options)	
Mandatory Placement		

Student Management
(Course Load, Attendance, Standards, Probation Period, Student Record Data)

demand for success. This macro instructional system, the parts of which are drawn from reality, then represents a model for an institutional approach to a well-organized instructional system design.

Proactive Preenrollment

Jefferson Community College (JCC) in Louisville, Kentucky, which was recently named one of the five most outstanding teaching community colleges in the U.S. by a panel of nationally known experts, developed a Recruitment, Retention, and Attrition (RRA) project in 1978 to attack an institutionwide problem: Tremendous growth had turned attention away from the individual student and focused it on the larger numbers of students (Roueche, Baker, and others, 1983). Public relations efforts and strong retention strategies had come to be largely ignored; the actual and potential results were frightening. A sobering look at the potential of an enrollment downturn and increasing attrition challenged the college to make significant changes, most particularly in the areas of communication with potential students. JCC's RRA project has, among other things, improved communication with potential students—a major initial step toward retaining large percentages of its newest students.

Formerly, once a student had applied for admission to JCC, he or she would receive a prompt response about acceptance. Then there would be no other correspondence until announcement about orientation—a usual time lapse of three or four months. Now, the admission letter is sent, and it is followed within two weeks by a letter from the division chairperson of the student's intended major and a letter from the student's academic department. The expanded capabilities of a potentially impersonal system for communicating with students help to personalize their contacts with the college. Students' responses indicate that the additional notice that they receive from JCC increases their commitment to completing enrollment and spending time in the environment.

The concern for the student who demonstrates interest in JCC by seeking admission has been expanded to embrace the entire community of potentially interested learners. Thus, the classified staff at JCC recently focused an entire staff development day on improving the important role that they play in student advising by providing accurate and proper information when students call, directing troubled or confused students to appropriate personnel, and calling ahead in order to personalize the experience further (Poole and Roberts, 1986). In short, attention to the most familiar technology—the telephone—has improved JCC's image and service.

Entry-Level Assessment and Mandatory Placement

Our national survey revealed that the large majority of colleges and universities were strongly in favor of mandatory assessment. However, respondents were not as solidly in support of mandatory placement

(Roueche and others, 1984). Surprisingly, we discovered that community colleges as a group put fewer "teeth" into placement policies than did four-year colleges and universities.

However, there were some notable exceptions. For example, Miami-Dade Community College, recently selected as the outstanding teaching community college in the U.S. by a panel of nationally known experts, has engineered a flexible institutionwide system that can accommodate wide student diversity (Roueche and Baker, 1986). One component of this system, the Comparative Guidance and Placement Program (CGP), requires students in college for the first time, students who have earned fifteen college credits or more, and students who wish to enroll in any math or English course to be tested in reading, writing, and computation. Results of the CGP test are used to place students in appropriate developmental courses and to restrict them to other appropriate course work and academic load.

Assessment becomes little more than a futile developmental effort if an institution is unwilling to make mandatory placement an instructional policy. Faced with the likelihood that basic skill courses will protract their academic or vocational programs, most students will choose to ignore any warning that the skill courses are crucial to their success in college and take their chances if left alone to do so. The key, then, is administrative support for the mandatory placement of students into the courses that assessment results indicate are necessary. Furthermore, directives for institutional evaluation of the results of mandatory assessment and placement should be in place.

Under the mandatory testing and placement policy at Miami-Dade, retention declined in the first year (from 50 to 45 percent), but it increased in the following year. Enrollment levels did not vary during the implementation of the system. Statistics describing relationships between successful completion of developmental courses and persistence and graduation revealed that a student's chances of graduating were nine times better if he or she took prescribed developmental courses than if he or she did not (Roueche and Baker, 1986).

Mandatory assessment of entry-level skills is the key to identifying low-achieving students before they enroll in any courses that demand reading, writing, and figuring skills. Standardized tests are useful for identifying major problem areas. In-house tests are strong follow-up devices that can provide instructors with accurate analysis of specific skills deficiencies. In any event, assessment must provide some solid direction for specific development activities and reflect the options that the institution offers for basic skill development.

In regard to mandatory placement, our survey indicated that every type of college and university was strongly in favor of mandatory placement. However, open-door community colleges were singularly and surprisingly lenient in this regard, with as many favoring voluntary as favoring mandatory placement in all three skill areas.

As mentioned before, the key is administrative support for mandatory placement of students into courses designed to provide appropriate skill development, but it carries with it a serious professional requirement—not to ignore the obvious legal obligation—to offer courses that provide instruction in the skills actually demanded in the regular academic and vocational courses in which the student will eventually enroll. Academic advisers must have the authority to make these courses conditions for enrollment.

Basic Skill Development

Beyond the basic teaching skills courses designed to bring students to acceptable performance levels, there appears to be a growing concern that the development levels achieved in these courses will be further raised in regular course work—that active instruction, performance, and evaluation of reading, writing, and figuring skills will continue across the curriculum. As we found in our study, institutions that conduct audits of courses in which students are likely to enroll and that develop a generic set of skills to which their developmental courses teach report significant cognitive links between what are typically and unfortunately discrete, disjointed courses (Roueche and others, 1984). As one important aspect of a macro system approach, discovering what is demanded across the college curriculum serves to identify strengths and weaknesses in the institution's instruction and expectations of student performance. In other words, at what levels of proficiency, if at any, are students required to demonstrate basic skills outside the developmental courses?

Institutional responses to this issue have identified a significant lack of attention to improvement of writing skills. Writing is now, as it has been for some time, one of the basic skills around which there has been much confusion and uncertainty regarding the particulars of instruction and evaluation. Writing-across-the-curriculum plans have become a popular topic. The strategies needed for implementing these plans and for embracing increased demands vary considerably across institutions, and instructional technology appears in varying degrees of importance and sophistication. But, two of the major concerns remain consistent: instructor insecurity around the teaching of composition and the increased time needed for the evaluation of students' writing. Two helpful systems examples for combating these common instructional issues come to mind: Wandah (Friedman, 1984) and Camelot (Anandam, 1984).

Wandah (Writing Aid and Author's Helper) is a comprehensive microcomputer-based system for improving composition developed at UCLA in the Word Processor Writing Project, which was funded by a grant from the Exxon Education Foundation (Friedman, 1984). This system helps students to plan and organize their ideas, transcribe them into print, and edit and revise them. It has three major components. First, the word processor has an on-line tutorial, an extensive menu system, and specially labeled function keys. One important feature is the availability of "windows" that permit the student to view an outline of his or her paper in one window and portion of the text in another or two parts of the text at the same time. Second, it contains prewriting programs to help students summarize their main ideas, overcome urges to edit their work too soon, keep the writing process moving along, and select and organize arguments into usable outlines. Third, it contains revising aids that help students to revise for mechanics (punctuation, word usage, and spelling), style (analysis of sentence and paragraph length), and organization (directions for summarizing and improving transition). Wandah also provides a reviewing or commenting aid that allows other students, the instructor, and other reviewers to read the composition and make comments on it.

Camelot, a microcomputer-based system for individualizing information was developed at Miami–Dade Community College with partial funding from the Exxon Education Foundation (Anandam, 1984). Because information is not prespecified in Camelot, the system can be used to meet a variety of instructional needs. For example, to save time in evaluating individual student papers yet to maintain a personalized teacher-student relationship, "forms were designed which allow an essay reader to mark students' errors in writing. These forms, when processed by Camelot, produced individualized feedback letters consisting of detailed explanations for the specific errors marked in each student's essay. Of course, reading the student's essay still remains the teacher's responsibility, but writing the selected feedback for the various students falls into Camelot's domain" (Roueche, 1984, p. 3).

Articulating with Subsequent Courses

The large majority of our responding institutions reported ongoing articulation with subsequent courses about the skill demands in writing and mathematics, while lesser numbers reported articulation about reading demands.

If the student is required to enroll in and successfully complete skill courses, there should be conclusive evidence that the courses have made a difference in the student's subsequent academic performance. Furthermore, the college should be able to document that students who are deficient in basic skills cannot pass other courses without first completing the required developmental work. Skill deficiencies left unchecked and unnoticed in regular courses signify low levels of skill expectations—certainly skill requirements that are significantly lower than those traditionally expected in college-level work.

As surely as basic skills cannot be taught outside some meaningful context—that is, there must be a mechanism for linking what the student is doing to why—any course content is easier to grasp when there is some unifying sense of utility and value. The academic freedom to decide course content and instructional methodology does not carry with it the authority or the option to disregard the larger reason that the course exists and that students must enroll. Instructors must know more than what they expect of students, both on the skill and the content levels. They must have a working knowledge of how their course fits into the larger academic scheme of the student's program of study.

This is a crucial item or linkage element in such a systems approach, and colleges must provide documentation and evidence on the academic credibility just stated.

Instructional Prescriptions Based on Assessment

If the assessments are to be effective in offering direction for instruction, they must accurately identify specific deficiencies, and they must be keyed to the actual content of the skills course. Instructors of basic skills should then be able to prescribe an instructional approach for the student; that is, the work assigned to individual students should depend on assessment information, not on group norms or predetermined course content and schedule.

In addition, the student's progression through course work is determined by a series of appropriately timed miniassessments designed to monitor student performance, signaling when to move forward and when to take advantage of the opportunity to repeat instructional units and review for alternate tests. An instructor's routine knowledge of how students negotiate course content and the reading and writing demands is one important way of preventing the information gaps that can result either in student confusion and potential failure or in student dependence on memorization and short-term information gains.

Our survey indicated that a significant majority of all institutions supported the use of prescriptions for designing course work for individual students.

Content-Based Instruction

An individualized instruction system approach, under which instruction is designed around the notion of teaching to individual learning differences, is content based. That is, early on there has been a concerted effort to identify what ought to be taught and to whom. For example, in the basic skills area, an audit should be conducted of courses in which most students will eventually enroll. That audit should produce a fairly well-defined set of generic reading, writing, and figuring skills. Once these generic skills have been identified, they can be used to direct curriculum and instruction decisions for the basic skills courses. In regular courses, such an audit would well serve the instructor who valued producing a gestalt of learning for the student—that is, a knowledge of how the content of any one course fits into the required larger core of courses. This knowledge could be central to students' enthusiasm for developing important skills and learning content; it will provide important cognitive links between what are typically and unfortunately discrete, disjointed courses.

All forms of instruction rest heavily on demonstration of competencies and these competencies have been identified at the outset prior to specific learning activities. The competencies or behaviors that are prescribed outcomes of the instruction should be shared with students, preferably in statements of objectives for small units of instruction. Larger objectives—those normally associated with course outcomes—are best shared as the student nears completion of the course for prescription, when he or she can more easily visualize and positively embrace the larger set of accomplishments.

Our survey documented that, while most institutions approve and support individualized instruction in the form of self-paced modules, there is little effort to provide alternatives for students with different learning styles. In this time of interest in individual differences and in the use of instructional technology to expand students' options, it is sadly curious that relatively few institutions have adopted a modern approach to instruction and instructional system planning at this level.

Exit Testing

The use of exit tests to determine a student's readiness to proceed to regular or other academic or vocational courses suggests, first, that there is a prescribed set of outcomes intended for the student and that instructors can use these outcomes to measure student performance levels, and second, that instructors know what skill and content demands will be made on their students in subsequent courses and that they have accordingly designed their curriculum and instruction around these identified demands. (While it is not a frequent practice, some institutions allow students to leave the course—prior to its scheduled completion date—with grade in hand once they have successfully fulfilled all prescription requirements and passed any exit tests.) According to our survey, more than one half of all institutions use the exit testing component in basic skills courses to determine a student's readiness to enroll in regular college courses. Of the skills courses, writing and mathematics were most commonly characterized by the use of exit testing.

Managing Student Behavior

College policies that limit the number of hours and types of courses that students may attempt until they have had an opportunity to prove themselves academically help to prevent lost time in classes that the student cannot pass and loss of student motivation to continue.

While less than the majority of institutions in our survey reported limiting course loads in light of outside responsibilities and academic deficiencies (interestingly, community colleges did not vary significantly from institutions attracting smaller numbers of working adult students), a healthy majority did set attendance standards for their students.

On the micro, classroom level, Miami-Dade's Camelot system allows instructors to track the individual student's progress, regardless of the diversity and size of the class, and to plan for corrective instruction. Camelot's capabilities allow it to meet a wide variety of instructional, counseling, prescription, task assignment, and other needs. It can be used to tailor instructor feedback to students to reflect individual student characteristics—for example, reading level, level of mathematical ability, age, computing specifics, previous courses taken, and mother tongue. It can analyze students' responses to objective tests and the results of teacher-marked assignments from different perspectives, it can compare the individual student's learning status with established course criteria, and it can compose and print individualized feedback letters for each student. In effect, it can be used to improve any educational setting that needs to reduce student diversity and number to a manageable learning situation and that recognizes the importance of the teacher-student relationship.

At the macro level, institutions that propose to assume some responsibility for student success stay tuned to the individual student's progress and provide direction and support when institutional criteria and feedback indicate that there is a problem. These colleges acknowledge the complexity of implementing such a system, but here we offer some models that are proving to be worth the effort.

The Standards of Academic Progress (SOAP) system at Miami-Dade Community College is used to monitor student performance and control credit load (once the student has completed seven credits). Feedback to the student includes warning, probations, and suspension notices. Evaluations of SOAP's effect on student persistence indicate that the suspension rate has declined each term for the last four. Studies on the pool of students eligible for suspension show that the decline results from improved student performance, not from increasing numbers leaving the college. Furthermore, the SOAP policies around load restriction and other support measures are successfully affecting the intended outcomes of increased student performance, persistence, and success (Rouche and Baker, 1986).

Miami-Dade's Academic Alert System sends letters of individualized information to all students concerning their academic progress approximately six weeks into the term. Students note that the early warning gives them time to get the help they need in order to improve their performance. Evaluations of the Academic Alert System indicate that students who sought assistance after receiving the warning showed increases both in performance and in grade point averages, while those who received a warning and declined assistance showed decreases in both areas. Similar findings were reported when groups of students receiving early warning were compared with groups who received no warning at all.

At Miami-Dade, the positive correlations between attendance and academic performance have promoted further monitoring of student attendance patterns. At Urbana College in Ohio, this significant relationship has prompted similar monitoring efforts so that nonattendance patterns are detected early. Researchers at the Center for the Improvement of Teaching and Learning at the City Colleges of Chicago determined that a strong relationship existed between attendance and final course grade. Copies of this report, accompanied by a most telling histogram, were distributed to instructors; many shared it with their students (Easton, 1984). All in all, successful student management hinges on the institution's determination to make and implement policies that do more than exert random and/or inconsistent pressure on students to behave in ways that we professionals know are in their best interests.

Conclusion

While teachers and administrators in American colleges and universities have been grappling with the literacy problem for the last decade or more, they now have at their disposal a vast array of technological possibilites that can be used to improve both student persistence and student achievement. Our model highlights the macro elements to be considered when the systems approach is applied to the problems faced by low-achieving students. Technology plays a role in the systems used for gathering important data and communicating them to the individuals who can progress most by it. This technology—which ranges from the relatively familiar to the latest in design and function—can help colleges to assure quality in all courses and programs without closing the open door.

References

Anandam, K. *Effectiveness of a Computerized Academic Alert System on Student Performance.* Miami-Dade Community College, 1984. 43 pp. (ED 245 741)

Easton, J. Q. "Attendance and Achievement." *Innovative Abstracts*, 1984, *6* (30) (entire issue).

Friedman, M. P. "Wandah: A User-Friendly Instructional System." *Innovation Abstracts*, 1984, *6* (16) (entire issue).

Hertling, J. "Test Score Decline Caused by Drop in Academic Rigor, Study Finds." *Education Week*, December 12, 1984, p. 10.

Poole, D., and Roberts, A. "Professional Development for Classified Staff." *Innovation Abstracts*, 1986, *8* (6) (entire issue).

Roueche, J. E., and Baker, G. A. "The Success Connection: Examining the Fruits of Excellence." *Community, Technical, and Junior College Journal*, 1986, *56* (5), 47-56.

Roueche, J. E., Baker, G. A., and others. *Beacons for Change.* Iowa City: American College Testing Program, 1983.

Roueche, J. E., Baker, G. A., and Roueche, S. D. *College Responses to Low-Achieving Students: A National Study.* Orlando, Fla.: HBJ Media Systems, 1984.

Roueche, S. D. (ed.). "Camelot: An Individualized Information System." *Innovation Abstracts,* 1984, *6* (14) (entire issue).

John E. Roueche is professor and director of the Community College Leadership Program at the University of Texas at Austin.

George A. Baker III is associate professor of educational administration at the University of Texas at Austin.

Suanne D. Roueche is senior lecturer in educational administration and director of the National Institute for Staff and Organizational Development at the University of Texas at Austin.

The authors received the Council of Universities and Colleges 1985 Distinguished Research Publication Award for College Responses to Low-Achieving Students, *which is cited in this chapter.*

The issue of copyright poses serious questions in the area of educational media, particularly for those who produce or copy nonprint media.

Copyrights Revisited

George H. Voegel

Ten years ago, on the eve of the passage of the revised Copyright Act (October 19, 1976), community colleges were somewhat preoccupied with who owned what, when, and where. These concerns were reflected in the numerous publications (for example, Voegel and Fischer, 1975), workshops, and conference sessions on faculty ownership, college rights, and such practical concerns as when one can tape off-the-air broadcasts.

Now, many colleges are again concerned about who owns what, when, and where. Again, numerous articles are being written, and presentations are being made at conferences, and workshops on faculty rights and on such practical concerns as when one can make copies are being offered. So, what has happened? It still looks like the colleges have the same concerns—or do they?

Yes, they are the same concerns, but the problems are different. In 1975, the colleges were concerned with audio and videotaping off the air, use of films on closed circuit and other television systems, and use of the copier in the library. The new copyright law created some definitions and parameters under which educational institutions and libraries could make copies. Fair use was explained, and new classes of works that took much of the new technology into account were created.

The Copyright Act

When the Copyright Act became effective on January 1, 1978, the new classification system for materials (expressions of ideas) had five categories. Class TX, Nondramatic Literary Works, is a broad category that includes all types of published and unpublished works written in words or in other verbal or numerical symbols. Examples include fiction, nonfiction, poetry, periodicals, textbooks, reference works, directories, catalogues, advertising copy, and compilations of information. Class PA, Works of the Performing Arts, includes published and unpublished works prepared for the purpose of being performed, either before an audience or indirectly "by means of any device or process." Examples include musical works (and words), dramatic works (and music), pantomimes and choreographic works, and motion pictures and other audiovisual works. Class VA, Works of the Visual Arts, consists of published and unpublished pictorial, graphic, and sculptural works. It includes pictorial or graphic labels and advertisements as well as "works of artistic craftsmanship." Examples include two- and three-dimensional works of fine, graphic, and applied art; photographs; prints and art reproductions; maps and globes; charts; and technical drawings, diagrams, and models. Class SR, Sound Recordings, is used for published and unpublished works where the claim is limited to the sound recording itself and in cases where the same claimant is seeking to register both the sound recording and the musical, dramatic, or literary work embodied in the sound recording. Sound recordings are works that result from the fixation of a series of musical, spoken, or other sounds. However, the audio portions of audiovisual works, such as film sound tracks or audiocassettes accompanying slide or filmstrip presentations are considered as integral to the audiovisual work as a whole. Class RE, Renewal Registration, covers renewal regardless of the class in which the original registration was made. It can only be made during the last calendar year of the first twenty-eight year copyright term, and it extends protection for an additional forty-seven years, for a total of seventy-five years. Forms for each registration class and other information can be obtained from the Copyright Office, Library of Congress, Washington, D.C. 20559.

The Copyright Act also describes the fair use doctrine. Generally speaking, fair use allows the copying of a limited amount of material without permission from, or payment to, the copyright owner where the use is reasonable and not harmful to the rights of the copyright owner. In the business world, being harmful to the rights of the copyright owner means denial or loss of sales. Any copying to avoid additional purchases is an infringement beyond the fair use concept for educational and research purposes. The law provides for actual or statutory damages, which are waived for libraries and nonprofit educational institutions when the copying is under fair use guidelines, of $100 to $50,000 plus legal costs and, when the copying is for willful private gain, for criminal action subject to a $10,000 fine, one year of imprisonment, or both.

Fair use guidelines for books and periodicals were developed after the Copyright Act became effective. Single copies for classroom use (chapter in a book, newspaper or periodical article, short story, poem, essay, graphs, pictures, and so forth) and multiple copies for classroom use must meet three tests: the test of brevity, the test of spontaneity, and the test of cumulative effect, and each copy must include a notice of copyright. Brevity is defined as copying only 250 words or not more than two pages of a poem; at least 500 but not more than 1,000 words *or* 10 percent, whichever is less, of any prose work or complete article, essay, or what have you of less than 2,500 words; and two pages *or* ten percent of the words found in "special" works, by which the Copyright Act means works in which language and pictorial illustrations are combined. Spontaneity is defined as action at the instance and inspiration of the individual teacher and under conditions in which both the decision to use the work and the moment of its use are determined by considerations of maximum teaching effectiveness that would make it unreasonable to expect a timely reply to a request for permission. Cumulative effect defines or limits the use of copies to one course in the school where the copies are made; one short poem, article, essay or two excerpts per author; not more than three excerpts from the same collective works or periodical in one class term; and not more than nine instances of multiple copying per term. Copying shall not be done to replace collective works.

These guidelines, as well as the required statements about copyright violations posted on copy machines in libraries and other college locations, have done a great deal to alleviate the concerns of educators about their liability in this area of copying. By the way, the tests do not apply to sheet music. The copying of this type of material is very restrictive, as several colleges learned when they circulated copied materials to the members of their band.

While the complications involving the copying of printed materials just about reached an operable status quo, the copying of nonprint media seems to be an area where confusion reigns. When and under what conditions a college could copy video programs kept making national headlines in the late 1970s and early 1980s. Sinofsky (1984) has detailed the legal background. Improvements in the technology and a drop in the cost of video tape recorders (VTRs) changed the dynamics and "mix" of the radio, recording, film, and television industry.

Guidelines for Off-the-Air Recording

Another important extension of the "fair use" doctrine focuses on off-the-air taping. Numerous organizations, such as the American Council on Education, the American Library Association, the Association for Educational Communications and Technology, and the National Education Association, as well as many media industry associations helped to develop

some guidelines for off-the-air recording of broadcast programming for educational purposes. The guidelines went into effect in October 1981. They are presented here in tabular format.
1. The guidelines apply only to off-the-air recording by nonprofit educational institutions.
2. The copy can be made as the broadcast is being transmitted and kept for forty-five days after recording; it must then be erased.
3. The copy can be used once by the individual teachers, and it can be repeated only once during the first ten school days within the forty-five day period.
4. The copy can only be made at the request of individual teachers. No more than one recorded request per teacher per program is permitted, no matter how many times the program is broadcast.
5. A limited number of copies may be reproduced subject to all provisions governing the original recording.
6. After the first ten school days of the forty-five day period have expired, recordings may be used only for evaluation purposes, not for "student exhibition" or nonevaluative purposes.
7. The copy does not need to include the entire program, but the content of recorded programs may not be altered, nor can recorded programs be merged in order to make anthologies or compilations.
8. All copies must include the copyright notice as it was recorded.
9. Educational institutions are expected to establish appropriate control procedures so they can maintain the integrity of these guidelines.

Copyright Royalty Tribunal

Congress also created the Copyright Royalty Tribunal in 1976 to oversee the rate structure of the Copyright Act. This little-known agency of five commissioners conducts about seventy hearings a year under its authority to adjust cable television's compulsory license fee schedule. Rather than negotiating prices individually with every programmer or copyright owner, the cable industry, under the Copyright Act, pays compulsory license fees for broadcast programs that it takes off the air and retransmits. While there is no direct connection to education, this tribunal, according to Montgomery (1985), is causing friction between the cable industry, which says that the rates are too high, and the motion picture industry, which say that the rates are too low. The indirect implication for education lies in the operating costs for local cable operators and in the ability of local operators to provide adequate educational access to local cable resources. As costs for cable operators go up, non-revenue-generating activities will be cut back. One has only to look at the current downscaling of channel availability, the limiting of access to studios, and the cable company's performance as a mere "pass-through" electronic service. It is possible the tribunal may become embroiled in the controversy over off-satellite transmission and recording. Again, from a copying standpoint the impact will only be indirect for community colleges.

New Technological Copying Concerns

The electronic evolution (revolution?) ushered in by the new technologies—mini- and microcomputers, laser and optical videodisc equipment, fiber optics, networking, satellite telecommunications, and the proliferation of video tape recorders for personal use—raises new concerns. Such concepts as off-the-air taping of telecourses and current event programs, the "picking" of programming off satellites, and the copying of computer programs from floppy disks seem to be the contemporary areas of concern.

Section 117 of the Copyright Act, which was added in 1980 to cover the copying of computer programs, states in part that "it is not an infringement for the owner of a computer program, provided: (1) that such a new copy . . . is created as an essential step in the utilization of the computer program in conjunction with a machine and that it is used in no other manner or (2) that such new copy . . . is for archival purposes only and that all archival copies are destroyed in the event that continued possession of the program should cease to be rightful." Any exact copies prepared in accordance with the provisions of this section may be leased, sold, or otherwise transferred, along with the copy from which such copies were prepared, only as part of the lease, sales, or other transfer of all rights in the program. "In consideration of a computer networking situation, the concern is whether the copying is an essential step for the utilization of the program in conjunction with a machine." A program that is designed to interact with computers in a network and may reproduce of itself is clearly legitimate. Copying a master disk and putting the copies in multiple classrooms for their networks is not permissible under Section 117.

Computer-related activities present a particularly difficult problem for community colleges as well as for education in general. Many colleges have microcomputer labs or learning resource computer centers, which check out software to students and other users, have study groups linking into computer networking, and so forth.

The agreements and other procedures developed within the computer software industry are directed primarily at other businesses and do not take into account the usual educational use of materials in the classroom, lab, or library setting. The software industry outlook concentrates on the business office environment and on protecting its products from piracy. Software developers do not want program disks to be copied for other office users, they want additional sales, so they either encode the disks for use on only one machine, or they require purchasers to sign severe contractual agreements. This activity may be justified but it ignores the usual educational use and LRC-type controlled circulation of computer program materials.

While some companies are beginning to loosen up toward the educational sector, most still describe their materials as for use in the business environment. Only where software is described as designed for a multiuser environment can computer programs be used in a networking situation and stay within the copyright protection.

Action to Be Taken

What can community colleges do? First, they can make sure that their own procedures related to the use of coyrighted materials are in order. That is, they can follow the fair use doctrine, they can observe the guidelines for off-the-air recording of broadcast programming for educational purposes and the fair use guidelines related to the copying of books and periodicals, and they can abide by any contractual agreements already entered into with any vendor or lessor.

Next, they can be assertive in defending the notion of the educational use of materials and the fair use doctrine against industrial and business inroads in this area. Reed and Stanek (1986) suggest that LRCs note on their purchase orders that the software being purchased is meant to circulate. These authors suggest the wording PURCHASE IS ORDERED FOR LIBRARY CIRCULATION AND PATRON USE. Industry views copyright from an entirely different perspective, and if educators will not defend their own appropriate use of materials, they should not expect industry to defend such use for them. Stanek (1986) contains additional useful information.

Developing appropriate software collections is another area to investigate. Probably various departments at many colleges already have a variety of computer software programs, while at some colleges attempts are being made to organize the software into some kind of collection. Identifying the software to buy is becoming easier thanks to proliferation of software reviews in the literature, but most producers are very reluctant to allow their software to be previewed.

A clear statement of collection scope and policy is needed. Consideration must be given to programming, languages, multiple copies, locally produced and public domain software, compatibility with equipment, and the multiuser environment. All this presents a challenge for cataloging. Guidelines for the descriptive cataloging of microcomputer software are being developed by the Committee on Cataloging Description and Access of the American Library Association's Resources and Technical Services Division. A number of colleges have developed their own cataloging systems.

The Copyright Act of 1976 did not address computer programs. As already mentioned, Section 117, the Computer Software Copyright Act of 1980, clarified it somewhat by giving the owner the right to make copies as needed to use the program or for archival purposes, but the owner does not have the right to make copies to give or sell to anyone else. Nothing in the law prohibits the educational lending of software. As long as a good faith effort is made to prevent illegal copying, colleges are protected from liability by Section 504 (c) of the Copyright Act.

Each college LRC or library should set up procedures for the reviewing of software contracts and site licenses to make sure that they are not too restrictive for educational use. Basic software loan policies and procedures that allow students and others to use the software while protecting the rights of software producers and publishers have been outlined by Demas (1985). All colleges concerned with computer software collection problems should consider the following recommendations: First, colleges (or their libraries, instructional computer centers, or labs) should try to limit their purchases of software for loan use to programs exempted from the provision that a particular copy of a program may only be used with a particular machine. Second, software should remain in the appropriate center; however, printed documentation may be circulated outside the center or even outside the college. Third, patrons should sign or acknowledge a statement on copy protection when they borrow programs or other software. Fourth, copyright warning notices must be posted at every computer work station or location where the illegal copying or software could occur. Another option is to place a copyright warning label or sticker on each disk envelope or program cover. Fifth, the original disk should be stored as a backup, and only a working copy should be loaned, unless special vendor agreements stipulate otherwise. Last, programs designed to break the copy protection codes on disks should not be allowed to be used in college facilities or on college equipment.

Still another area in which community colleges need to be active is the area of contractual agreements. The cooperative purchase or leasing of telecourses and other materials has been an effective arrangement for both colleges and industry. Under a cooperative agreement, a fee for the master set of materials and a specified number of copies or duplications is written into the contract. Such arrangements allow groups of colleges or consortiums to purchase materials and make multiple copies for additional fees. Industry is satisfied because such arrangements enhance the original sale concept and reduce the potential for unauthorized copies. The colleges are satisfied because they can now individually afford copies of materials that they could not have gotten otherwise.

The computer industry has yet to discover the approach already taken by film and telecourse vendors, but according to Gillin (1985) there are signs that some vendors are beginning to loosen up. One of the major areas of concern is whether the software is used under some leasing agreement or through site licensing. Since computer software is relatively useless unless an entire program is copied (see the paragraphs on the fair use earlier in this chapter), the criterion "the amount and substantiality of the portion used in relation to the copyrighted work as a whole" is a serious factor. Copying the whole work, except as defined in the off-the-air guidelines, seems to be prohibited by the fair use concept as it applies to books and periodicals. Copying small portions of a program is within the intentions of the fair use doctrine, but the resulting copy is not likely to be very useful. Wholesale copying is not permitted by the fair use doctrine unless the program is described as for a multiuser environment.

Summary

In summary, the legal and guideline support structure has moved forward with the technology at a fairly rapid pace over the last ten years, especially when one considers that it took Congress seventy-one years to change the Copyright Act. With the advent of multiple-copy guidelines for prints, guidelines for off-the-air recording, multicopy leasing and purchase agreements for films and videotapes, such as telecourses, and some positive indicators in the computer technology field, it appears that the legal and guideline support structure that will enable education to cope with issues related to the copying and use of the newer technologies will be in place within a few years. Colleges will still need to attend to their own ownership and related policies regarding faculty and other staff development of materials as appropriate to all these technologies. It remains for the community colleges to apply these appropriately in using the technology.

References

Demas, S. "Microcomputer Software Collections." *Special Libraries,* 1985, *76* (1), 17-23.
Gillin, P. "Vendors Shucking Copy Protection." *PC Week,* 1985, *2* (12), 4.
Montgomery, H. "CRT: Small 'Cog,' Big Clog?" *Cable Television Business,* 1985, *22* (3), 42-47.
Reed, M. H., and Stanek, D. "Library and Classroom Use of Copyrighted Videotapes and Software." Insert in *American Libraries,* February 1986.
Sinofsky, E. R. *Off-Air Videotaping in Education.* New York: R. R. Bowker Co., 1984.
Stanek, D. "Videotapes, Computer Programs, and the Library." *Information Technology and Libraries,* 1986, *5* (1), 42-54.
Voegel, G., and Fischer, M. "Copyright and Ownership of College-Developed Materials." In G. H. Voegel (ed.), *Using Instructional Technology.* New Directions for Community Colleges, no. 9. San Francisco: Jossey-Bass, 1975.

George H. Voegel is dean of educational services at William Rainey Harper College in Palatine, Illinois.

A recent survey demonstrates that the new and old can coexist successfully within the framework of educational technology as coordinated by the systems and structure of the learning resource center.

Educational Technology in Multicampus Community Colleges: A Decade of Change

Gloria Terwilliger

Technological change is a dominant feature of today's society. The most prominent emerging technology is, of course, the computer, which is permeating the consciousness of our society through mass communication. In the McLuhan tradition, the media are the messages, and the messages are being produced by the media. Decision makers in education and training have been responding to the urgency of the messages. Institutional priorities have been rewritten in order to commit massive amounts of funds for purchases of computer hardware and software, personnel, and maintenance. The adoption of large-scale high technology is straining the financial resources of our colleges and drawing funding away from existing instructional supports and technologies.

Community college presidents, boards, and faculty members are reexamining their missions, priorities, and resource allocations in the face of changing enrollment patterns, national priorities for the strengthening of secondary education, and competition from short-range training offered by proprietary schools and industrial training programs. Soaring tuition-costs, partly generated by the expense related to providing high technology

G. H. Voegel (ed.). *Advances in Instructional Technology.*
New Directions for Community Colleges, no. 55. San Francisco: Jossey-Bass, Fall 1986.

for student and administrative use, are threatening the community college commitment to open access and to low-cost comprehensive programs. The revision of resource allocations affects all areas of the college as units compete for a share of available funds.

Programs in data processing and computer science require the tools of their technology. Engineering, drafting and design, the natural sciences, and the social sciences all have increasing needs for computer applications to instruction in order to meet the realities of these applications in the world of work. Resource needs of some high-tech training specialities cannot be met through normal budgeting procedures and allocations, and institutions are seeking other sources of funding to support these requirements. Curricula are being reexamined. George Vaughan (1984), president of Piedmont College (Virginia), speaks to these problems: "Some community colleges are already beginning to rethink the commitment of vast amounts of resources for conferring degrees in such highly specialized fields as laser technology, robotics, and any number of 'high-tech' specialities which . . . appeared to be tailor-made for the community college . . . Instead of specializing in a single high-tech field, it will likely be necessary for community colleges to offer a technical program including work in a number of areas but a specialty in none . . . [conferring] . . . a two-year 'liberal technical' degree."

Technology and the LRC

The introduction, application, and use of educational technology in the nation's community colleges have been supported by staff and facilities in the learning resource center (LRC). The development of these supports has been influenced by a set of guidelines prepared by practitioners that was published and endorsed by the three major national associations concerned with learning resources in the community colleges: the American Library Association, the Association for Educational Communications and Technology, and the American Association of Community and Junior Colleges. These guidelines for two-year learning resource programs (American Library Association, 1972) have served as descriptive standards for effectiveness, efficiency, continuity, and access. Learning resource center leadership has spurred the application and use of instructional technology, including micrographics, photography, cinematography, magnetic sound recording, television, videocassettes, and other audiovisual supports. There exists a long record of experience in the administering of instructional systems, including learning laboratories designed for group and individualized instruction, technical instructional supports, video services, and telecommunication systems, which vary in their sophistication and complexity as a function of instructional demands and institutional budgets.

Most of the systems and procedures for instructional technology were developed between 1965 and 1975, a period of substantial federal funding and state and local support for community colleges. Once the equipment and basic systems were in place, refinements in use, replacement of obsolete equipment, and development of materials collections characterized the next several years. The process of instructional development, that is, faculty-developed units of instruction predicated on an instructional systems approach and produced by the audiovisual specialists, was heavily supported at some institutions and reached its peak in the mid to late 1970s. The impact of the computer revolution, which coincided with changing enrollment patterns, has resulted at many institutions in the reordering of priorities away from individually supported instructional development projects.

Impact on Learning Resources

Until recently, community college learning resource centers with expanded programmatic thrusts have commanded a substantial share of institutional funds. The current pressures on institutions to divert large portions of their budgets to the purchase of computer equipment, software, and supplies and to the provision of staffing for this technology have inevitably resulted in a redistribution of priorities. Funds to support ongoing LRC instructional development programs and audiovisual equipment and related software have diminished. A study by the Association for Educational Communications and Technology (Albright, 1983) analyzed budget trends for media services in private and public colleges between 1977 and 1983. The study showed that 30 percent of the public college media centers had received no budget increases since 1977. During that period, a high rate of inflation was further decreasing the buying power of dwindling budgets.

The equipment, techniques, production facilities, materials, and staff required to support a comprehensive process of educational technology were delineated and defined during the 1970s by a task force of the Association for Educational Communications and Technology. At that time the statement of needs and requirements included only a nominal reference to computers and computer-assisted instruction (CAI). The domain of educational technology had been created by the introduction of audiovisual devices to the instructional process, and it was raised to a discipline by the application of educational psychology and the so-called "systems approach." Theoretical and practical work by audiovisual specialists and instructional technologists laid the groundwork for the adoption of computer technology, which began to gain momentum in the late 1970s.

Current Trends in Educational Technology at Multicampus Community Colleges

The impact of changing technology on learning resource centers is often the subject of discussions at meetings, workshops, and conferences. A formal assessment was carried out by surveying the LRC directors at fifteen multicampus community colleges: Macomb Community College, Warren, Michigan; San Diego City College, California; Los Angeles Trade Technical College, California; Peralta Community College District, Oakland, California; Pima Community College, Tucson, Arizona; William Rainey Harper College, Palatine, Illinois; Northern Virginia Community College, Fairfax, Virginia; St. Louis Community College, Missouri; Dallas County Community College District, Texas; Chicago Citywide Colleges, Illinois; Montgomery Community College, Rockville, Maryland; Portland Community College, Oregon; Miami-Dade Community College, Florida; Anchorage Community College, Alaska; and Cuyahoga Community College, Ohio. The questions were designed to collect observations and impressions rather than quantitative data, since the emphasis of the survey was on trends and changes during the past decade.

The directors were invited to comment on changes in use, shifts in technological emphasis, and budget support for standard audiovisual equipment and materials; video equipment and installation; instructional systems, including assessment testing and instructional design; and production of audiovisual television instructional materials. Directors were also asked to comment on their LRC organizational structure and to specify administrative responsibilities beyond traditional library and media services. Last, they were asked to describe the status of academic computing at their college and to identify any LRC role and responsibilities.

Survey results indicate that the use of standard media equipment (films, overhead projectors, slides, and so forth) has increased since 1975 in proportion to institutional growth. Declines in use at some colleges were said to reflect cuts in materials and staff support budgets. Budget support for standard technology has diminished at many of the reporting institutions as a result of increasing competition for funds between the providers of traditional services and new services. Exceptions were noted in the reporting sample at some of the West Coast colleges and at two community colleges heavily invested in telecourse production.

Macomb Community College's report on the use of standard media equipment is characteristic of the colleges sampled. Macomb indicates an overall increase in the number of pieces of equipment delivered to classrooms. The use of sixteen-millimeter film is decreasing and the demand for three-fourth-inch videocassette and half-inch equipment is increasing. (All institutions polled reported an increase in the use of videocassette technology, with a decrease in the use of sixteen-millimeter film.) Existing films in frequent use are being replaced with video prints as resources permit. A decline in the use of opaque projectors has been offset by increased use of overhead projectors. Few faculty request reel-to-reel tape recorders, and there has been a decrease in requests for record players. The current demand is for audiocassette players.

Most of the LRC directors indicated an increased emphasis on the use of instructional objectives in curriculum development and an increased use of assessment testing. It was reported that there is a trend toward the development of exam questions and test item banks supported by microcomputers, district mainframe computers, or both.

Two major CAI systems are being used in the institutions. The City Colleges of Chicago have used the PLATO system for a number of years. In a recent pilot project in Chicago, PLATO served as a delivery system for telecourse materials to students. An electronic mail capability was developed to facilitate communication among students and faculty and to track and monitor student progress.

The Alexandria campus of Northern Virginia Community College and the Phoenix Campus of Maricopa Community College both use TICCIT (Time-shared Interactive Computer-Controlled Information Television). TICCIT is designed to deliver full courses or modules, with built-in learner control, student tracking, monitoring, and progress reports. Electronic mail is a standard feature. At Northern Virginia, standardized testing on TICCIT has been used for the freshman sequence of biology since 1980 and in data processing courses since 1984. The TICCIT system supplies randomized tests and analysis of test items.

Most of the colleges sampled report that staff development programs for the improvement of non-computer-based instruction have become limited in scope. The educational technology model, which was predicated on the use of a support team consisting of instructional designers, educational psychologists, and content specialists, has not been generally adopted at campus levels. It is more likely to be the method employed for the development of telecourses and other space- and time-free forms of instruction that are centrally staffed and administered. Comments relating to the diminished status of instructional design highlighted the lack of specialized staff at the campus level, lack of funding, and faculty resistance.

Obsolete Forms of Media

Respondents were asked to specify the forms of instructional media that had been discarded. Dial-access labs have been abandoned. Language labs have not flourished, having been replaced by portable cassette technology. Some have been redesignated *audio labs;* these labs are used by multiple disciplines, and their resources have been augmented by loan and duplication of cassettes—a development that reflects needs of commuting students. Programmed instruction on autotutors is virtually extinct, as is Super Eight film, the Language Master, the Didactor, the speech compressor, reel-to-reel tape, and sound-on-slide. These devices and others described by Finn (1972), which supported early efforts to individualize instruction, now represent outmoded technology. They have been superseded by audio- and videocassette technology, by the use of slides and slide-tape presentations, and by the growing use of computers.

The report from Macomb Community College provides an insight into the demise of distance distribution systems for film, another technological system of the late 1960s. Contributing factors are the change over from film to video and the desire expressed by faculty to retain control of the medium in the classroom in order to be able to pause and discuss, to review, and to use selected portions of a film or video presentation.

Production of audio and video materials at the campus level has diminished at some institutions, sometimes as a result of centralized production of telecourses. However, St. Louis College reports that all production is done at the campus level and that campuses provide production assistance to the district office. More than one respondent noted that local production was limited to individual uses in classrooms. Most institutions reported that they are now almost exclusively purchasing commercially produced instructional media in all formats.

These sample responses and comments indicate that a standardized set of basic instructional media supports has emerged, consisting primarily of film, audio- and videocassettes, slide and slide-tape, and the overhead projector. Faculty have adapted their instructional style to these supports, and they have themselves developed a wide array of technical skills, ranging from the operation of video equipment to the design and production of overhead transparencies and other media formats for classroom purposes.

Telecourse Utilization

The use of telecourses varies considerably. In 1984-85, the Dallas County Community College District, with about 100,000 students at seven campus locations, enrolled approximately 4,000 students in fourteen telecourses each semester. Chicago City Colleges reported that approximately 4,000 students (out of a districtwide student base of 125,000) were enrolled in television courses in spring 1985, including courses for credit, adult and continuing education, English as a second language, and GED training; both broadcast and campus-based videocassette formats were used. At Portland Community College, about 2,700 students enroll in telecourses each year. Miami-Dade Community College reports telecourse enrollment at about 1,500 students per year. Anchorage Community College enrolls 1,300 students districtwide, and there is extensive use of teleconferencing.

Montgomery Community College reported that about 900 students enroll in telecourses each year. At Pima Community College, approximately 450 students were enrolled in twenty telecourses during spring 1985. The St. Louis district reported an enrollment of more than 1,000 students in telecourses. At William Rainey Harper College in suburban Chicago, about 300 students register each semester for approximately six courses, which are delivered in a variety of formats: broadcast, videocassette, and cable television. Harper College also reported that 72 percent of their telecourse students owned their own VCRs.

Adapting to Computers in Instruction

All the colleges reported increasing use of microcomputers and the establishment of microcomputer labs. At four—St. Louis Community College, San Diego City College, William Rainey Harper College, and Northern Virginia Community College—computer labs are staffed and supervised by the learning resource center or equivalent component. At Miami-Dade, business and data processing control the discipline applications; the LRC controls the instructional support services for the labs. A similar pattern is found at Anchorage.

St. Louis Community College reports the highest saturation and use of computers among the institutions surveyed, with major funding thrusts providing personal computers, minicomputers, and mainframe equipment and software. These new technologies have been in place for several years, and they have stimulated faculty use of instructional design services, thereby increasing faculty awareness of the importance of instructional objectives. Funding for microcomputer purchases has had high priority at St. Louis. In mid 1985 the library remained without automated systems, but media services had developed an automated inventory and circulation system. (Information about library automation was not solicited in the survey, which was limited to audiovisual instructional applications; the information was supplied by the director in comment form.)

A planning document developed by the directors of learning resources at Northern Virginia Community College (Northern Virginia Community College, 1981) predicted that campus learning resource centers would evolve as the logical centralized location for computer-assisted instruction and interactive computing. The document pointed out that supports and activities for computer labs—proctors and lab assistants, testing, record keeping, distribution of related information, use over extended time periods, and preparation of reports—are typical LRC tasks and procedures. Emphasis was placed on the value of consolidating equipment for ease of maintenance as well as for security, deployment of cross-trained staff, and interdisciplinary access. The ordering and cataloging of microcomputer software parallel the standard bibliographic procedures developed for other audiovisual media. It was therefore recommended that responsibility for interdisciplinary academic computing laboratories be an LRC responsibility. Specialized labs, such as computer-aided design (CAD) and graphics, may not be appropriate for interdisciplinary use and therefore should usually be the responsibility of the instructional department.

In 1985, the Consolidated Computing Laboratories at the Alexandria campus of Northern Virginia Community College included forty-seven MUSIC (Multi-Users System of Interactive Computing) terminals and three twenty-two-station microcomputer labs in adjoining areas. These interdisciplinary labs serve the campus computing needs, with peak occupancies in the evening hours and on Saturdays. The labs can be handled by two instructional assistants with work study help except during peak periods, when additional staff are scheduled. The labs are normally open 90.5 hours per week; that level increases to 100 hours or more at the end of each quarter.

Implications of the Responses to the Survey

Survey feedback suggests that support for instructional technology in the nation's community colleges continues to be one of the primary responsibilities of the comprehensive learning resource center. During the late 1960s and well into the 1970s, media specialists, librarians, and educational technologists on LRC staffs guided the selection of appropriate instructional equipment and resources, trained faculty in the use of the technology, and encouraged instructional improvement through demonstrations, orientations, and workshops. All these activities are reported to be still going on in some form or another.

The LRCs leadership role has for the most part been structured as a partnership between the instructional faculty and staff of the learning resource center. Analysis of learning strategies and instructional problems and identification of solutions have been a mutually shared responsibility. However, survey comments pointed out that the advent of microcomputers on campus has created a tendency to disregard existing partnerships.

The learning resource center provides interdisciplinary access to facilities, resources, and equipment, thereby expanding use and minimizing purchasing and utilization costs. LRC staff have developed multiple competencies and a broad perspective on available resources, as demonstrated by the various survey examples. The integrated LRC has become a balanced and complex network of instructional supports, based on assessment and evaluation of use, focused on quality of resources and validity of materials in the achievement of instructional goals, and engaged in projecting for future needs.

The faculty, LRC staff, and administration at each community college need to reexamine the partnership role regarding the various technologies highlighted in the survey, and they need to develop an appropriate partnership mix for the implementation of microcomputing in the instructional process. If they do not, the results could be financially costly and instructionally devastating.

The Future Is Linked to the Past

The increasing pressure for massive investments in computing equipment, coupled with changing enrollment patterns and the loss of many federal supports for both students and programs, is causing college administrators to review closely the allocation of funds. Each mid-level administrator has new cause to assess operations, analyze trends within his or her unit, review statistical and report data, and be prepared to make effective recommendations for budget allocations and position responsibilities. Many survey comments from LRC administrators indicated that staff were being retrained to support computers on campus.

In developing rationales for the retraining and reallocating of existing staff, the value of the role of media professionals should be articulated. Media educators have been trained to be innovators of change in education. According to George R. McMeen (1983, p. 15), "Professionals in the field of educational technology have an important role in helping education make the transition to the technological age. Their perspective is a valuable one, for it is broad enough to encompass more then one technology and to envision new directions for institutional change."

The instructional support services have been developed by LRC professionals, whose background may include theoretical training in instructional systems, learner characteristics, task analysis, curriculum design, and material evaluation. This background is eminently transferable to microcomputer software. For example, a comprehensive and functional set of evaluative criteria for selection of self-instructional materials was developed in the mid 1970s by Hecht and Klasek (1975) for use at Moraine Valley Community College in Illinois.

Microcomputer software currently flooding the market is similar to the media that have been marketed for more than two decades. Those forms of media suffered in their initial developmental state from a comparable eagerness to capture the commercial market, a factor that seriously affected their quality. Criteria for the evaluation and selection of software programs used for computer-aided instruction (as differentiated from applications programs designed for interactive business and data processing purposes) do not differ substantially from the earlier set of instructional material criteria. Course objectives, alternative learning activities, clarity of instructions, motivation, reference manuals, assessment instruments, and product revision continue to be key points in the evaluation of software for selection.

Most of the instructional software available for microcomputers at the time of this writing can be categorized as instructional enhancement and "skill and drill." These programs are able to use the sophistication of computer technology to supply tutorials with differential feedback, which Sydney Pressey's (1927) primitive "teaching machines" attempted to provide as early as 1926. Three decades later, Norman Crowder attempted to design programs with branching feedback ("intrinsic programming"), but the technology of the fifties was unable to support the theoretical design.

The inclusion of computers in the configuration of the LRC services is in keeping with the mission and purpose of the LRC. Adoption of the technology as another LRC service builds on existing staff skills and knowledge and combines resources to strengthen instructional support services. It is of vital importance, however, to retain and support the standard, widely used, and validated basic instructional media services that are critical to the instructional program and that can be most effectively utilized and subsidized in tandem with the growing use of computing equipment and services. LRC professionals will know, as they have in the past, when certain instructional resources and equipment become obsolete.

Today, instructional supports are being developed in new formats: floppy disks, videodiscs, and compact discs. As survey responses show, the new and the old can coexist successfully within the framework of educational technology as practiced through the systems and structure of learning resource centers which allow them to support the instructional goals of the faculty and the college.

References

Albright, M. J. *The Status of Media Centers in Higher Education.* Washington, D.C.: Association for Educational Communications and Technology, 1983. (ED 242 306)
American Library Association. *Guidelines for Two-Year College Learning Resources Programs.* Washington, D. C.: American Library Association, Association for Educational Communications and Technology, and American Association of Community and Junior Colleges, 1972.
Finn, J. D. *Extending Education Through Technology.* Washington, D. C.: American Association of Colleges of Teacher Education, 1972.
Hecht, A. R., and Klasek, K. R. "PAS: A Tool for Developing or Selecting Self-Instructional Materials." *Audiovisual Instruction,* 1975, *20* (4), 28.
McMeen, G. R. "The Academic Challenge of Technological Change for Leadership in Educational Technology." *Educational Technology,* 1983, *23* (12), 15.
Northern Virginia Community College. *The Learning Resource System: A Comprehensive Analysis.* Annandale: Learning Resource Centers, Northern Virginia Community College, 1981.
Pressey, S. L. "A Machine for Automatic Teaching of Drill Material." *School and Society,* 1927, *25* (647), 549–552.
Vaughan, G. B. "Balancing Open Access and Quality: The Community College at the Watershed." *Change,* 1984, *16,* (2), 40.

Gloria Terwilliger is director of learning resources at the Alexandria campus of Northern Virginia Community College in Virginia.

Small community colleges are ready to take full advantage of advanced instructional technologies. Declining prices and cost savings of cooperative purchasing will help.

Limited Edition: Small Community Colleges Adapt to New Technologies

Carl D. Cottingham

Limitations may be our best friends, because they require imagination. Small community colleges are quite accustomed to dealing with limitations—limited enrollments, limited staff, limited funds for innovation and problem solving. This chapter describes how some small colleges are coping with changing instructional technology. It reports on a sampling of current use of the newer instructional technologies in small-sized community colleges, addressing such issues as the underlying philosophies toward use of instructional technology in the classroom, use of new methods of delivering instruction outside the classroom, and use of technology to expand the services of the learning resource center (LRC) or library. The information presented here was gathered from seven colleges of 2,500 FTE enrollment or less: John A. Logan, Carterville, Illinois; Bee County College, Beeville, Texas; Lake City Community College, Lake City, Florida; Mesabi Community College, Virginia, Minnesota; Paducah Community College, Paducah, Kentucky; Somerset County College, Somerville, New Jersey; and Walla Walla Community College, Walla Walla, Washington.

Just as creative architects see limitations as their greatest challenge, many LRC administrators in small community colleges have learned to view things in the same way. As these colleges approach the use of instructional technology, they typically must proceed cautiously, and they have less opportunity to experiment than larger institutions do. The small colleges have learned to do their homework before recommending a new course of action that involves technological application to instruction. The background work typically involves surveying the literature, calling or visiting other community colleges, and, most of all, good old-fashioned critical thinking.

Of course, it is to be hoped that much thought precedes the purchase of technology at any community college, small or large. For example, a decision to provide microcomputers in the learning resource center or in a generic open computer lab demands careful consideration, because our resources are limited. Since computers are basically a one-to-one device and since they are still more expensive per unit than other audiovisual equipment, there must be a significant advantage in this technology over others if we are to justify its cost. What can this technology do that is not being done as well now by traditional teaching and by less expensive instructional technology?

Use of Instructional Technology in the Classroom

All colleges surveyed reported heavy and increasing use of videotapes and computers in classroom instruction. The use of sixteen-millimeter films and thirty-five-millimeter filmstrips seems to have decreased in the last five years, as the cost of videotapes and playback equipment has dropped and the quality has improved. One college is involved in teaching by telephone, and one uses a satellite down-link to receive educational programs for transmission over a local cable system.

Some of the colleges have learning laboratories in the LRC that directly support classrooom instruction by providing students with opportunities to use audiotapes, videotapes, filmstrips, and other media. Typcally, these learning labs in the small colleges are centralized and serve all college programs and curriculum. Services may include test proctoring, telecourse assistance to faculty and staff, tape duplicating, and test scoring. Some LRCs that do not have a separate learning lab-type facility provide such services within the library area.

None of the colleges surveyed gave faculty direct assistance in the use of computers to manage instruction by providing such services as test scoring, storage of test data, calculation of grades, or test preparation. Six reported either that such assistance was planned for the near future or that individual departments or instructors were already providing it.

New Instructional Delivery Systems

What technologies are being used to provide new instructional delivery systems outside the traditional classroom format? Responses indicated that television-based courses were the most popular. Four colleges were offering between two and five telecourses every semester, either by making tapes available at the college and at viewing centers in the community (public libraries are the most popular sites) or by duplicating tapes for students, cablecasting, and/or broadcasting.

Learning resource center directors in small community colleges report that telecourses offer three clear advantages: First telecourses provide a realistic way of expanding the variety of curricular offerings without large expense and delay. The limitations of a small faculty make this an important consideration. Second, telecourses make it possible to reach new students whom time or distance problems and family or work obligations have prevented from taking part in campus-based activities. Third, telecourses offer an important flexible scheduling element that may allow many students (especially part-time students) to take the courses that they need when they need them.

The colleges that have not used telecourses see their value, but they have not been able to use them for one or more of three reasons: lack of up-front money for leases, equipment, and broadcast charges; limitations of administration time to manage the courses; or lack of interest among faculty or administration.

It is clear from my own experience at John Logan College (Illinois) that the small community college cannot realistically offer telecourses without getting involved in a cooperative effort with other colleges and universities. When professional development efforts, program purchase or lease costs, and broadcast charges can be shared, the use of television-based courses can become cost-effective.

Courses delivered by radio, newspaper, and telephone also offer the advantage of overcoming time and distance barriers, but they are used minimally by small community colleges. Mesabi Community College (Minnesota) offers one telephone course per semester in cooperation with Bemidji State University.

Computer Use for Instruction

All colleges surveyed reported use of computer-assisted instruction as a method of delivering instruction to students outside the traditional classroom setting. However, if we take a closer look, we see that these uses of computers for teaching are not all that new in regard to the delivery system. As a rule, they are placed in laboratory settings, not in traditional classrooms. In such areas as physics, foreign language, business, and drafting, this is not so different from existing practice, but now we see computer labs being used in such areas as English and music. This represents an important integration of technology into the instructional process of many colleges and it has far-reaching implications for the future. Perhaps more than any other technology that has so far been brought into teaching, it will affect the role of instructors in relation to the delivery of instruction. Most instructional administrators at the colleges that I contacted are convinced that the computer will be able to deliver certain instructional functions extremely well. They are typically trying to respond to the requests of their faculty and adminstrative staff for the purchase of computers. Development of the faculty does not appear to be a large problem, since many are learning about computers on their own and taking advantage of in-service training opportunities with little or no encouragement from the administration.

LRC Collections and Services

As the new technologies have affected the strategies and methods of teaching, they have also changed the LRC collections and services of small community colleges. All colleges sampled have videocassettes in their collections. The content of these tapes include telecourses used in credit courses and tapes used in the regular classroom to supplement instruction. Many are reporting a switch from sixteen-millimeter film to videotape because purchase costs are lower and there are fewer maintenance problems with the playback devices. Tapes of general interest or of an entertainment nature are not provided by any of the colleges sampled. All but one of the colleges sampled provided videotape playback units in the LRC area.

About half of the colleges surveyed have been adding microcomputer software to their collections. Some report sizable collections of computer software used in instruction, but in all cases the collections are housed in computer labs outside the LRC operation. Only two of the colleges sampled seemed to be making a serious effort to coordinate and centralize software programs through the LRC. In small community colleges, this would seem to be the most efficient way of making the college's software collection available to students and faculty. The goal, in my opinion, is a centralized, cross-discipline collection with an adequate number of microcomputers in a very accessible location that is open for extended hours. Neither the collection nor the facility would replace the computer labs in science and business; they would supplement them. Also, they would open the way for instructors in other areas of the curriculum to begin using computers outside the classroom.

In response to the question, How has technology affected the services provided by LRCs?, most of my contacts mentioned the use of bibliographic data bases and networking of library computers. Since most small or medium-sized community college LRCs have small collections, they view the computerized networking of libraries as a breaking down of distance barriers and a means for bringing about a significant increase in the efficiency of information transfer between libraries. Five of the seven LRCs in my sample used a computer network to make interlibrary loan requests. These networks ranged in scale from a few libraries within a two-county area to a state or even larger system using the OCLC network. Such a service allows students and other patrons of these LRCs to search the collection of all the interconnected libraries from any one of the libraries. The interlibrary loans can generally be handled much more rapidly than they can by using the telephone or mail. Interlibrary loan requests are made via electronic bulletin boards, which can also be used for other messages or questions. These devices have had the very positive effect of bringing small libraries closer together. LRCs that participate in a computerized library network may also have patron-access terminals that completely replace the traditional card catalogue. Surprisingly, only one college in the sample offered patron-access terminals, and it still maintains the card catalogue as a backup. Two colleges were planning computerized catalogues for the near future.

Two colleges were using national data bases, such as Dialog, as an added service to their students and faculty. Literature searches that before could be done only in a large research library can now be performed via telephone lines from a library-based terminal. There is a charge for the on line computer and the long-distance telephone time, but most libraries find that patrons are quite willing to bear such charges. One college in the sample was also offering computer-based library instruction and consultation in the production of software.

Perhaps the area in which small community colleges have shown the most imagination in dealing with the problems imposed by limited resources and isolation is the area of cooperating with other institutions and agencies. The two types of cooperative efforts that were most prominent in my sampling are computer library networks and learning resources cooperatives.

Computer Library Networks. Computer library networks can be simple networks connecting computer terminals together in order to show bibliographic data, more complex systems in which a central minicomputer stores bibliographic information in a central data bank and services many libraries, or highly sophisticated regional or statewide systems that can handle hundreds of libraries on line. In addition to providing bibliographic information, these networks typically provide electronic interlibrary loan ordering and other message capabilities, and they sometimes include cataloging services, circulation services, and acquisition services as well. The colleges involved in these networks report that there have been problems, but they feel that the advantages of increased services to patrons and increased cost-effectiveness make the networks worthwhile.

Learning Resources Cooperatives. Learning resources cooperatives can be formally established with bylaws and incorporation status, or they can be very informal. Cooperatives typically meet monthly or bimonthly in order to share information, conduct professional development activities, and do cooperative purchasing and leasing.

The Southern Illinois Learning Resources Cooperative, of which John A. Logan College is a member, is a formally established not-for-profit corporation consisting of fourteen institutions of higher education. Eleven institutions are public-supported community colleges, but only two enroll more than 2,500. The other three colleges are four-year institutions. This cooperative began in 1979, and it was modeled after the highly successful Northern Illinois Learning Resources Cooperative. (For more information on cooperatives, see Chapter Three of this volume.)

For the small community colleges, the cooperative or consortium can be a very valuable resource. Cooperative purchasing can bring about better discounts, professional problems can be shared and sometimes solved by other members of the cooperative, and time-consuming and expensive professional development can be shared. Telecourses provide a good example of the benefits of such cooperative arrangements. Without the sharing of ideas and leases, broadcasts, and master taping expenses, the smaller colleges could not have implemented telecourses. All seven colleges sampled were active in some type of cooperative with other colleges or community agencies. The small community college has much to give and much to gain by reaching out cooperatively to those in its area when considering application of instructional technology.

Conclusion

Small community colleges have used imagination to overcome their limitations as they cautiously and methodically consider applications of technology to problems posed by limited staff, limited finances, and isolation. As technology continues to develop, costs are reduced, prices drop, and cooperative sharing of costs increases, we see the small colleges ready to take full advantage of instructional technologies.

Carl D. Cottingham is dean for learning resources and continuing education at John A. Logan College, Carterville, Illinois, where he has developed an exemplary full-service learning resource center over the past seventeen years. He is the telecourse coordinator for the Southern Illinois Learning Resources Cooperative and he has served in numerous regional and state leadership positions in the library and audiovisual field.

Despite the application of technology, classroom instruction has changed very little, and while accountability in terms of contact time remains intact, little progress is likely to be made in enhancing the human aspects of teaching.

Technology for Education: Promises and Problems

Kamala Anandam

The technological revolution that we face in education today did not happen overnight. It was set in motion by inventions that began fifty years ago. The momentum of its impact was felt initially to lie within the limits of human comprehension, but the feeling now is that we are being overwhelmed by the information explosion unleashed by technology. This feeling has not blinded us, however, to the application of computer technology across a spectrum of activities, ranging from manning spaceships to helping a blind person to read. The accelerating capabilities show no sign of leveling off, and I doubt that they ever will because, as Alvin Toffler (1980) has pointed out, the mental power of humanity will expand along with them. As long as the mental power keeps expanding, people will continue to challenge themselves to accomplish extraordinary feats with technology. Out of a galaxy of such feats, only some have become useful and affordable for education.

The distance between technological invention and educational innovation is nothing to be alarmed about as long as we educators recognize the gap and attempt to bring the two together. To do so, however, requires an honest analysis of promises and problems stimulated by technology, which are likely to run deep into the fabric of our educational practices.

This chapter describes some promises and problems that computer technology poses for educators. The description intentionally excludes the uses of the computer as a career tool in such disciplines as secretarial science, business data processing, and architecture. This type of computer use hardly raises a controversy among educators, but it does involve finding the money to equip labs with the necessary hardware and allocating the time to train our faculty to use them.

The Leading or Trailing Edge of Technology

Individuals, whom I place at the leading edge of technology, claim that the technological revolution is sensational: Technology makes information available at our fingertipes; technology makes distance and time irrelevant to teaching and learning; technology increases productivity and cuts costs; technology makes us smarter, better human beings; technology is the great equalizer of the human race. Since technology is empowered to accomplish all these things, the bewildered proponents of the leading edge ask what is holding the educators back. They appease their frustrations by predicting the demise of educational institutions that do not wake up to the technological revolution. While there is some truth to each of these perceptions, those at the leading edge, who include many specialists in technology, seem to undermine the human context in which technology has to function. What becomes clear, when the human context is considered, is that one cannot afford to be engulfed by technology, because it might cloud our vision and mar our mission. At the same time, one cannot dismiss technology as a fad, because it is not.

Let us face it: Technologically it is possible for faculty to teach and students to learn without ever having to assemble in a particular room at a specified time. Imagine for a moment if that possibility were to become a reality. Should it happen? Some hold to the opinion that we have no choice, since the technological revolution is well under way, as exemplified by telecourses and other distance learning offerings, and that the deschooling of society (Illich, 1983) has begun. Others feel that, since humans are gregarious, they will always have a need for group interaction. Between these poles, the more realistic projection is that some of the educational activities that we now conduct in classrooms will become individual pursuits, while others, perhaps new activities, will become worthy of group interactive process.

This more realistic projection is associated with the trailing edge of technology. Those at the trailing edge are knowledgeable about the technological breakthroughs, and in many instances they exhibit a greater global understanding of technology than do those at the leading edge. Those at the trailing edge ask such questions as, How can we use technology to help humans become more human? They realize the extraordinary power of technology to enhance the human condition in the physical, intellectual, and social context, and they wish to exploit technology toward these useful humanistic ends. They seem to experience a nagging concern, however, about the absence of thought about differentiating the activities that are best carried out by humans from the activities that are best carried out by technology.

If we look more closely at the claims of leading edge enthusiasts and the concerns of trailing edge educators, we can see more clearly the promises and problems that are prompted by technology. I believe that an institution can recognize the promises and confront the concomitant problems by identifying the individuals at both edges of technology and by facilitating a friendly confrontation between them. Even if the confrontation becomes unfriendly at times, one can expect some gain as the leading edge is tempered by the trailing edge and as the trailing edge is tested by the leading edge.

Refinements in the Uses of Technology

Computer technology offers educators the opportunity to shift their focus from teaching to learning. Traditional classroom instruction has led us to believe that, because we know (or think) we do a good job of teaching, it is the students who are either capable or incapable of learning. With the uses of computers to date, we are increasingly asking two questions: Do computers make a difference? When do they make a difference? In other words, we are willing to question the medium. Attempting to answer some of these questions has led to some positive indicators (Fisher, 1983): First, information delivered in a classroom during a semester can be delivered by computers in a matter of hours or minutes. Second, computers are perceived as consistent, patient, and fair (human qualities that we cherish highly) by student members of minority groups. Third, computer-based instruction is more effective at raising achievement among low-and high-achieving students than it is among students of average achievement. Fourth, computer-based software that is integrated into the curriculum has a better chance of yielding positive results. Fifth, computer-based education leads to improved attendance, increased motivation, longer attention span, and significant positive change in student attitudes.

Early studies of computer-based education were not this clear in their results because the technological applications were still in their infancy and the investigations themselves were unrefined. However, subsequent studies (Anandam and Kelly, 1981) seem to point to the contexts under which technological instruction is useful. Unfortunately, the proliferation of microcomputers tends to overrun the need for sophistication and selectivity in applying technology to learning. Consequently, the hodgepodge of hardware and the array of incompatible software raise a problem that is complicated by the issue of obsolescence. Nevertheless, explorations and experiments must continue in order for us to span the spectrum of possibilities. I fear that if we seek standardization of hardware and software too soon, we may have to settle for mediocrity in both for a long, long time.

As we look for justifications for the use of technology in education, our search takes us in different directions. Some look for cost savings, and others look for time savings; some are contented with increased student motivation, and others strive for improvement in learning; some work for faculty development, and others work for institutional innovations. Motives aside, there is renewed hope that we in education can address the needs of the diverse student population, and this is a promise offered by the computer. As we manipulate this tool, we are beginning to look inward and question what we do, how we do it, and how we evaluate its use. These trends are slowly shifting the emphasis from things to processes, that is, from the question What should I get? to the question How should I use it?, thus moving toward a more meaningful use of technology.

Focus on Individualizing Instruction

Turning inward, no doubt, has led to some painful realizations, chief among them being our ineptness in conceptualizing the individualization of instruction. This problem is perhaps the most critical one for us in education. Should the same content be presented in different ways, or should the content be different for different students? Should we focus on course-specific content and requirements or on generic skills, such as problem solving and decision making, that cut across all courses? Should we treat independent study as synonymous with individualization? The search for answers to these questions calls for an evaluation of our present practices that is not palatable in all quarters. Therefore, some seek a solution by approaching the experts to find it for us, while others feel that retraining of the faculty and staff is a long-term solution.

The long-term solution has the advantage of providing an internal locus of control to the people who will use the technology. However, if we tackle the problems on our own, we encounter the problem of time, effort, and incentives. One has to spend hours evaluating existing software in order to select the appropriate programs. Do faculty have the time in our current settings? What about the question of remuneration? If an instructor has been hired to teach a certain number of courses and has done so for several years, will he or she be paid for the extra hours that are needed to incorporate technology into the process of individualizing instruction? Can community colleges afford to depend on the pioneering and altruistic inclinations of a few faculty to utilize technology fully? The problem for educators, then, is not so much technological as it is administrative and educational, and the solution lies in reorganizing the institutional environment so that it can address the questions of individualization of instruction.

Collaboration for Developing Quality

As educators, we know what knowledge our students need to have, and we know how we want them to use it when they graduate. We also want our students to become productive and valuable members of society. I realize that what we accomplish may fall sort of our ambitions, but that does not mean that we do not know what we want. Ironically, those outside education observe what is being accomplished and duplicate it in the computer. The result is that they underprogram the computer, because they underestimate the teaching-learning process. The trailing edge educators fear that if we get sucked into the graphically dazzling and economically feasible but educationally mediocre technology, we will lose sight of our ideals.

The creation of quality educational materials is no small matter, especially in the computer field, and we are forced to find ways of fostering collaboration among educational institutions and industries and among content specialists, learning specialists, and computer programmers—a collaboration long overdue. The emphasis here is on the joint intellectual effort, as contrasted with the financial sharing alluded to in the term *cooperation*. It is becoming apparent that without such combined intellectual force, which has already been demonstrated by television production consortiums, our chances of developing meaningful and useful software are rather slim. For instance, at the very elementary level, an individual faculty member's biases, preferences, and emphases are intertwined with the information presented in the classroom, but they are intolerable, if not plainly unacceptable to other faculty, when they are conveyed via a computer to their students. Yet, the heavy dollar investment required for development of computer software can only be justified by wide use. So, collaboration, a promise offered by computers, is almost a strategy of economic survival in the technological arena.

In my estimation, the collaboration should embrace both development and delivery of computer-based educational programs. Unfortunately, such things as institutional setting, organizational arrangements, class schedules, collective bargaining agreements, and individual personalities are not conducive to collaboration. This is a problem. An institution has seriously to consider hiring personnel to promote collaboration, whether it is inside or outside the institution, to work with faculty in designing and developing software or in evaluating existing software, and to assist faculty in integrating the programs into the curriculum (Anandam and Kelly, 1984). In other words, collaboration is to be actively cultivated, not left to chance.

Relegating Responsibilities to Technology

Computers offer the promise of separating the managerial aspects of teaching from teaching itself. By *managerial aspects,* I mean the institutional requirements of testing, grading, graduation, and so on. If we were to tally the number of hours spent in a year by all the faculty in an institution to administer and proctor tests, we might want to ask, Should faculty's time be spent this way? If the answer is no, we are ready to face the following questions: Is there a technological solution? Can a computerized test center manage the administration of tests? Can we have computers to administer the tests? Is it advantageous for students to take the test when they are best prepared for it rather than at a prescheduled class meeting? I present these questions on testing only to make a point that we as educators have to reexamine our teaching and related activities to determine which ones we wish to relegate to technology.

Imagine, if you will, a case in which "magic" is able to free faculty to teach—free the faculty from such nonteaching roles as policeman, record keeper, and disciplinarian; free the faculty to interact with informed, well-prepared, and eager students rather than lecture to students who may not be prepared to listen. Technology is the "magic" that can accomplish this by presenting information to students on an individualized basis and by monitoring and evaluating student progress.

In this scenario, technology delivers all the lectures, explanations, and demonstrations that usually occur in today's classroom. The students are given a set of questions and asked to find the answers by utilizing the technological delivery system. Of course, the presentations are interactive so that the students can use them according to their learning needs and any number of times to meet those needs. Peer group interactions are also encouraged by this technology.

What would the teacher do then? Since so much of what a faculty member does today has little to do with teaching, the scenario just sketched may give a sense that technology is replacing the teacher. This is not so. What it does, instead, is give the faculty an opportunity truly to teach—to engage in student-teacher interaction that can truly lead forth the student to a deeper understanding of what has been learned. Imagine a class situation where the students are the initiators of activities and not the teachers. It will be the students' responsibility to ask questions, express their doubts, dilemmas, and discoveries, and request the teacher to clarify or confirm or challenge their expressions. The teacher also takes the opportunity to share with the students what he or she is investigating or writing about—a kind of role modeling. This scenario sets the stage for a situation in which classroom time can be used for discussing the information presented through technology; today, that time is used principally to deliver the information. In this scenario, students take on a mentally active role for their learning. The classroom will never be the same.

In today's application of technology, it is sad to note that hardly anything seems to change in classroom instruction as we know it, and, while accountability in terms of contact time remains intact, little progress is likely to be made in enhancing the human aspects of teaching. How can an institution capture the unique and creative talents of its faculty and transmit these talents to students if not through human interaction?

This is the greatest promise of technology—to relieve us of mundane, repetitive tasks so that we will have time to attend to more humane activities.

Accentuating Human Qualities

It is true that the advent of mass education has caused teaching to be perceived as dissemination of facts and learning as recall of facts. This is not to say that teaching is devoid of inspiring interactions between faculty and students. As far back as we can trace, students have recalled vividly the inspiration and values that they derived from their teachers and proclaimed that their teachers brought out the best in them. Teachers, too, recall the incidents that gave them a great sense of sarisfaction: the sparkle in their students' eyes, their students' determination to succeed, their self-confidence, their concern for society, and their transition from "I'm nobody" to "I can make a difference." The critical question, then, is, How can technology be presented to faculty so that they can do more essentially human activities?

Humanness is recognized, nourished, and appreciated by humans. Technology can challenge, but I am not sure that it can inspire people. Technology can teach logic, but can it formulate our ethics? And, technology can expand our minds, but can it cultivate compassion? I guess, then, we have to delineate the educational activities that are uniquely nurtured by humans. When we do come up with a list of such activities, they should prompt us to expand our vision, examine our mission, and restructure what we will do and how we will do it. This is technology's greatest promise.

Conclusion

Technology hold promises and problems for educators. The promises and problems are unmistakably intertwined. We cannot capitalize on the promises without confronting the problems. As long as we rely on people, not technology, to deal with the promises and problems, we will be on the right track. Such reliance should encourage interaction between those at the leading and trailing edges of technology; interdependence of technological innovation and educational research; collaboration among content specialists, education psychologists, and technology experts; restructuring of the institutional environment; delineation of instructional activities that are best left to technology; and commitment to accentuate human qualities.

References

Anandam, K., and Kelly, J. "Evaluating the Use of Technology in Education." *Journal of Educational Technology Systems,* 1981-82, *10,* 21-31.

Anandam, K. and Kelly, J. "Taking Advantage of Emerging Educational Technologies." In D. G. Brown (ed.), *Leadership Roles of Chief Academic Officers.* New Directions for Higher Education, no. 47. San Francisco: Jossey-Bass, 1984.

Fisher, G. "Where CAI Is Effective: A Summary of the Research." *Electronic Learning,* 1983, *3* (3), 82-84.

Illich, I. *Deschooling Society.* New York; Harper & Row, 1983.

Toffler, A. *The Third Wave.* New York: Bantam, 1980.

Kamala Anandam is director of computer-based instructional development and research at Miami-Dade Community College in Florida.

We must engage in widespread and intensive discussions of the appropriate technological and human mix if we are effectively to serve the needs of community college students.

Instructional Technology Mix: Some Considerations

George H. Voegel

With each new gadget and each new advance in the practical application of a variety of technologies in our society by industry, new pressures are put upon education to upgrade and keep pace. Rarely has pressure for technological change come from within education itself. This chapter examines instructional technology from several facets in an attempt to get readers to consider ways of enhancing their decisions on the adoption of technological change for the betterment of student learning.

What Is Instructional Technology?

It is somewhat unfortunate that the generic view of instructional technology is oriented toward machines or equipment. Historically, that perception is fairly easy to put into today's context.

About one hundred and fifty years ago, the big technological change involved a shift from the hornbook (a notebook-size item made from animal horns that was used by individual students) to the slate board (blackboard) which, because of the mass media approach of its day, was primarily a teacher-controlled presentational piece of early technology. Change came slowly, and it was not until after World War II and the terrific expansion of school and college construction that blackboards became chalkboards that could be had in various shades of tan, green, or blue as well as the traditional black. However, from a teaching-learning standpoint, it was still he or she who held the chalk who controlled the presentation.

From the early 1900s to the early 1970s, many technological devices entered and left the classroom as the technology failed to achieve widespread adoption or as it was developed into something more useful as teaching tactics and strategies became more refined. Thomas Edison (1913) predicted that "books will soon be obsolete in the schools. Scholars will soon be instructed through the eye. It is possible to teach every branch of human knowledge with the motion picture. Our school system will be completely changed in ten years." Kurtz (1933) commenting on television in its infancy stated, "This new instrumentality [television] bids fair to become the most potent agency of universal education ever conceived. For, in due time, every home will have its own classroom, with professor, blackboard, diagrams, pictures, and students." Early advocates of educational television seemed to say the same thing. Lantern slides gave way to thirty-five-millimeter slides. Filmstrips fell from grace largely in higher education circles, but the opaque projector lingers on in the technological backwaters because it is easy to use: Just throw in the book, newspaper, or magazine, and there is your picture. Eight-millimeter film and its big brother Super Eight slowly yielded to the videocassette format. In the 1960s, the omnipresent chalkboard suddenly had to make way for the bright shiny kid on the block, the overhead projector. This particular item, which had been developed in the 1940s for military training, was slow to be adopted by regular education because of its price and the lack of materials. In the mid 1960s, the 3M company set the stage for large-scale adoption by introducing new thermoplastics for transparencies and by marketing a much cheaper projector. The situation then became one in which he or she who held the chalk, the transparency, and the light switch controlled the presentation. The learning research that had been conducted during the war on overhead and film use in instruction passed relatively unnoticed. Likewise, pioneering early efforts on individualized instruction did not see results until the 1960s when teaching machines with linear and branching program frames made their appearance. During the same time period, use of phonograph record players fell off in favor of reel-to-reel tape players, which quickly gave way to audiocassette players.

Exaggerated, unacceptable claims for the value and usefulness of radio in the 1920s, films in the 1930s, television in the 1950s, teaching machines in the 1960s, and dial-access technology in the 1970s are good examples of false prophecy and consequent disappointment. History has shown that technological devices, when introduced into education, have had marginal impact on the overall teaching-learning process. Due to the relative high cost, inconvenience of use, and general lack of adequate teaching materials for these early versions of instructional technology, effective utilization came about very slowly. The focus was on the cost, operating features, and procedures needed to use them. During this same period, state and federal funding was equipment oriented through a variety of title sources.

Scant or only sporadic attention was paid to the teaching-learning value of the materials that were being purchased, except in cases where the college was fortunate enough to have a professionally trained media specialist on staff who was knowledgeable about studies on the effectiveness of the use of such materials and technology. The teaching machines began to break down the machine orientation to instructional technology because of their heavy dependence on the teaching and learning materials designed for use in these machines. They were supposed to be equal to or superior to regular classroom instruction in the same content because thoughtful effort had been put into making each teaching frame a successful learning experience for the student. However, the information presented in frames was often so small or discrete that students lost interest or motivation. One spin-off of this effort was the marketing of numerous paperback instructional booklets that did not even use the equipment.

Several other efforts during this time were beginning to make their presence felt. The importance of instructional design and development in making teaching more effective over a broad spectrum of considerations were recognized. One leader in this field was Robert Mager (1962), whose ideas on the teaching process, as expressed in his books on instructional objectives, were widely discussed. A group lead by Benjamin Bloom (1956) examined the various facets or components of learning, and these ideas evolved into a series of taxonomies or domains that eventually led educators to the concepts of mastery learning. At the same time, numerous other educators and researchers were using the concepts of programmed instruction to lay the groundwork for computer-assisted instruction on large mainframe computers.

Current instructional technology thus has probably come to be seen as more than an instructional equipment approach. While most community college practitioners would take this view and while any in-depth discussion with them would reveal a reasonably comprehensive viewpoint about the instructional components of their teaching, it is likely that they still defer to an operational meaning of instructional technology that focuses on media, equipment, and materials.

Instructional technology should be understood in terms of the more encompassing concept of systems approach. The term *systems approach* refers basically to the utilization or application of four components: first, defining or determining as best as one can the students' learning characteristics and abilities; second, developing and sharing with students the learning outcomes (instructional objectives) expected of them in relation to course content (curriculum); third, determining and utilizing the procedures, processes, methods, and so forth that will instructionally help the students to get there; fourth, designing and continuously monitoring the measurement of student progress (by tests and so forth) to ensure that the interplay of the first three components is effective. (Chapter Four of this volume presents another version of this concept.)

Due to the maturation of community colleges and to the continuing professional development and growth of faculty and other staff, it is probably reasonable to expect that most people in the field will arrive sooner or later at a relatively close operational definition of instructional technology. However, nothing seems to stand still, and a contemporary intrusion that is confusing to many is turning attention away from the orderly evolution toward an instructional technology approach.

This intrusion comes wrapped in the terminology of high technology—high tech for short. High tech is roughly defined (turning back to an equipment orientation again) as the use of mini- and microcomputers in industry, at home, and in education. In a historical sense, we in education are seeing a modern and more sophisticated version of the efforts of early advocates to interest educators in immersing themselves in films, television, self-tutorials, teaching machines, or programmed instruction as the approach to instruction. The advocates of minis and micros are espousing *this* high tech as the new major instructional approach. In many cases, existing campus procedures and processes for the various media technologies that would appropriately apply to the new high tech have been ignored because people failed to comprehend the similarities between use of the new technology and use of the other technologies. The authors of Chapters One, Six, and Eight in this volume express similar concerns in their contributions.

It is to be hoped that community colleges will be able to settle into high tech and develop routine procedures, appropriate staffing, and other support. Such a development would enable us to turn our attention once again to the more important tasks of optimum implementation of the components of instructional technology suggested earlier.

Some Value Considerations

The application of instructional technology can be approached from several directions. Appropriate application of instructional technology should result in a marked improvement in the ability of learners to handle knowledge and make value judgments in an effective manner.

Our society has continued to produce a variety of devices and processes that allow information to be compressed, expanded, and transformed from one medium to another and that make it possible for thoughts and ideas to be expressed in almost any kind of delivery format. Such technological breakthroughs as thin-film plastics, which give us photographic films and audio- and videotapes; electronics, which gives us audio, radio, television, and other communication devices; and the microchip, which gives us the personal computer, are all adding new dimensions to our resources for education. Iconic, visual, electronic, analogic, digital, and various combinations of these as developed in software have provided the teacher with a vast array of resources that he or she can organize into a cohesive and effective expresssion of ideas, feelings, and thoughts. A combination of software resources and delivery systems with instructional and behavioral findings continues to give us new opportunities to define how learning will take place in our colleges.

Havelock (1963) has described the changing learning environment in ancient Greece as a shifting contrast between oral and written cultures. Prior to Plato, Greeks had memorized the poets, creating an operational wisdom of Homer and other poets and developing a tribal encyclopedia. Havelock observed that the poets had provided for all the contingencies of life—they were a sort of Ann Landers in verse. By Plato's time, the written word had created a new environment based on ideas that had begun to detribalize man. With the advent of the phonetic alphabet, classified wisdom took over, and education by classified data has been the Western educational program ever since.

With the new electronic technology, data classification yields to pattern recognition. When data move instantly, classification is too fragmentary. Thus, in information overload situations, people resort to the study of configurations or patterns. Today's technology and its environments succeed each other so rapidly that one environment makes us aware of the next.

We must clearly understand the limitations of technology. The technology expressed in today's devices will not solve the problems facing community colleges ten years from now. Technology can help only on the premise that it will enable teachers to do a better job of teaching. Most of us have already discovered the futility of changing goals as often as we change our technologies.

Changing Use of Technology

As noted in the first section of this chapter, each technology has its own unique set of characteristics. Those characteristics can lead to further use, or they can drive the technology from the teaching scene.

Ten years ago, for example, dial access, the audiotutorial approach, and individualized instruction were being examined or implemented in community college settings. How have these innovations fared in the past decade?

Bolvin (1975) reported on the success of Chester, a dial-access audio and video system used at Bellevue Community College that was receiving 30,000 calls per month from the community. It had the advantage of serving many users quickly, of facilitating individual learning, of giving direct access to learners, of allowing current topics to be included, and of having no time limits. The technology had three disadvantages: The initial cost was high, there were heavy programming and system maintenance demands, and learners could not always start at the beginning of a program. Clark (1985) reported to this author a decade later that Chester now resembles the old "Gunsmoke" character who had a bullet in the leg and limped badly. Technology has moved on, and Chester has not evolved accordingly. The college's resource allocations have been reduced, thus decreasing staff support for programming while maintenance costs go up. Chester still serves the community by receiving several hundred calls per month, but its use for instruction is limited, and the most popular use of Chester now is for listening to radio programs. Cable television technology has replaced Chester. Clark thinks that two lessons are to be learned: First, long-term maintenance and conversion costs must be considered; second, the cycle from innovation to practice gets progressively shorter, and replacement time periods are concomitantly shortened.

Parsons (1975) wrote on the technology of modular audiotutorial components (MATC) used at Hagerstown Junior College. The audiotutorial (A-T) system pioneered by Sam Postlethwait formed the backbone of this instructional approach. Since this was an instructional material ("software") approach that structured the sequence of learning steps prepared to facilitate learner attainment of specific competencies, it was not particularly equipment ("hardware") dependent. Thus, it was a process (systems technology) that required a great deal of teacher design and preparation to develop effective modules that would enhance the learner's progress. A decade later, Parsons (1985) reported that modularized instruction has become even more important and that it is being used in such community-based instructional settings as factories, prisons, police departments, and social service agencies. The A-T approach is still viable for the sciences, reading, mathematics, and engineering technologies, and it has increased the reliance on differentiated staffing. The emphasis is still on diagnosis, prescription, and individual pacing for the adult learner, and it has successfully increased retention rates. Faculty retraining with the new technology takes on the approaches of several models, such as the return to industry, instructional exchange, and internships.

The A-T approach just mentioned had its start in the early sixties in the biology lab of Sam Postlethwait at Purdue University. Modular instruction in an open lab that had been especially designed and equipped for the purpose, as well as motivational general assembly sessions, were part of the approach. Sam shared his innovative successes with anyone who showed an interest and many instructors in other disciplines, such as nursing and secretarial science, adopted his techniques. When asked to reflect on all this almost twenty years later, Postlethwait (1984) strongly emphasized that the underlying basis for A-T was solid and correct. The principles involved in the instructional design are tight. They are used in many other contexts besides that of the audio tape recorder. However, some educators jumped on the bandwagon without understanding what they were doing. Postlethwait had begun to replace the audiotape instructions with microcomputers before his retirement, and he feels that this is the direction in which instructional design should go. Indeed, he thinks that videodiscs clearly are even better. He concludes: "It could and should be an exciting time in education today. But, it seems to be difficult for teachers and administration to see the difference between the deliverance of subject matter and helping students grow. The difference is subtle but so very important when one begins to use various technological devices. In the final analysis, learning is something that is done by the learner, and devices, such as computers, tape recorders, videodiscs, and so forth, are only useful inasmusch as they bring the student into contact with subject matter in such a way that the student achieves some specific goals" (Postlethwait, 1984).

Where to from Here?

Are there any lessons to be learned from the past? Is there anything we can do now that would ease technological transitions, whether they involve hardware, software, or some form of systems configuration? What problems can arise from the implementation and use of new technology? What new directions can community colleges take to ensure the appropriate technological and humanistic mix in instruction? While there is no neat or precise set of answers to these questions, an observation or two can provide a perspective from which some judgments about technology can be made. Here is one suggestion: Take a reflective look at where (time, place, context, and so forth) conflicts, stress, or confusion over technological change occurred in society in general, in education, or at your college in particular. Try to think of the effects created by a particular situation. Was the situation caused by a lack of information, misperception, fear of being replaced, confusion over terminology, or a gap between early innovator and late adopters?

A general example of conflict and stress can be found in the simultaneous use of the wristwatch and airplane in World War I. Prior to that time, relative direction was always given in a nautical context related to a ship's compass: One was so many points off the bow, or something was sighted north by northeast. When the doughboys in the trenches quit using pocketwatches in favor of wristwatches, which were easier to see under the circumstances (up until that time wristwatches were for ladies only), and when their comrades in the skies began to describe dogfights in terms of relative bearings related to the watch face (one o'clock, three o'clock, and so forth), a new "system" came into being. It was expanded upon as a quick training technique in World War II, and it has been carried on in aviation ever since.

That analogic clock face (big hand, little hand) stuff, which served us so well, provided us with another relative directional set of terms: clockwise and counterclockwise. Everyone caught on quickly when asked to turn a bolt, nut, or screw in a clockwise direction, and the term was readily understood. Now enter the digital watches, which have only numbers, not hands. The generation that learns to tell time from digital watches is losing the context of clockwise and counterclockwise as relative directional terms. Nothing has come along to replace these terms yet, although there is some rather Teutonic terminology available—*widdershins* for counterclockwise, *deasil* for clockwise—but these will probably not be generally used.

With the advent of the microchip, the analogic functions are rapidly giving way to digital functions. The radio "dial" is no longer a dial, but rather a small window that displays the station numbers. Automobile speedometers are becoming digital. The newest in sound recordings are digital, done on a videodisc-type device. As many readouts are shifting from the more visual analogic toward the discrete digital number, a conceptual transition is occurring. The analogic, which took data readings from somewhere and translated them into a spatial, visual, or audio concept, was based on human spatial recognition patterns. You could look at the temperature gauge in your car and make a spatially relative judgment about the temperature of the engine. If these data are displayed in a numerical (digital) form, the conceptualization and the judgment of relative hotness or coldness must be different. Of course, we may be headed toward some ultimate technology that couples a voice synthesizer with digital microchip devices that would cause the voice synthesizer to say, "Engine too hot, stop the car."

The competing claims of analogic and digital display have now reached the level of controversy in commercial aviation. In the newest airplanes, such as the Boeing 767, the cockpit control systems have been so computerized that buttons can be punched that would cause the plane to take off from Chicago and land in London without human intervention. What the cockpit crew (pilot, copilot, engineer) really should do is being questioned. It has been suggested that the pilot's position be renamed *flight system manager*. The appropriate technological mix of humans and electromechanical systems is being questioned in airline operations.

The intensive introduction of computer technology into education is causing people to ask similar questions about the appropriate technological mix of human endeavors and electromechanical systems. The authors of Chapter Four in this volume are extremely sensitive to the student (human) side of the concern. The authors of Chapters One and Two are primarily addressing the systems delivery of instruction to students who are not on campus—distance learners. The authors of Chapters Six, Seven, and Eight are concerned about the appropriate technological mix within a campus setting. The authors of Chapter Three are really saying that changing or implementing the mix had become almost beyond the resources of one college and that sharing was a way of staying contemporary.

The audiovisual media, television, dial access, and teaching machines of the past have given us some insights into how education has reacted to suggestions for change in its technological mix. Currently, while the record is somewhat spotty, a number of community colleges have taken a far more comprehensive approach to the introduction of computers into the learning situation than has been taken in the past with other devices. They are showing a far more mature attitude in their approach to this form of technology than others have shown in the past to other technologies, but care needs to be taken to reach the appropriate partnership mix of faculty, learning resource center staff, and emerging microcomputer staff and supporters in order to make the most effective use of this technology.

Current campus leaders may have seen enough socioenvironmental *Titanic*s, such as the Three Mile Island and Chernobyl disasters, acid rain, toxic waste, and other pollution, from the technology that supposedly was built to serve society, not to destroy it. Perhaps they have realized we must engage in widespead and intensive discussions of the appropriate mix of technology and human resources if we are to serve the needs of students in their community and educational settings.

References

Bloom, B. S., and others. *Taxonomy of Educational Objectives*. Vol. 1: *Cognitive Domain*. New York: McKay, 1956.

Bolvin, B. M. "Using Technology to Serve Learning Needs of the Community." In G. H. Voegel, (ed.), *Using Instructioanal Technology*. New Directions for Community Colleges, no. 9. San Francisco: Jossey-Bass, 1975.

Clark, T. Personal communication of March 28, 1985.

Edison, T. "Interview on Future of Moving Pictures." *New York Times*, July 13, 1913, sec. 3., p. 8.

Havelock, E. A. *Preface to Plato*. Cambridge, Mass.: Harvard University Press, 1963.

Kurtz, E. B. "Interview on Television's Future." *New York Times*, January 17, 1933, sec. 9, p. 4.

Mager, R. F. *Preparing Instructional Objectives*. Palo Alto, Calif.: Fearon, 1962.

Parsons, M. H. "MATC Spells Instruction." In G. H. Voegel (ed.) *Using Instructional Technology*. New Directions for Community Colleges, no. 9. San Francisco: Jossey-Bass, 1975.

Parsons, M. H. Personal Communication of March 27, 1985.

Postlethwait, S. M. Personal Communication of October 3, 1984.

George H. Voegel is dean of educational services at William Rainey Harper College in Palatine, Illinois.

Drawing on the materials catalogued by the Educational Resources Information Center (ERIC), this chapter cites further sources of information on instructional technology at the community college.

Sources and Information: Instructional Technology at Community Colleges

Jim Palmer

A search of ERIC's *Resources in Education* and the *Current Index to Journals in Education* reveals four major themes in the literature on instructional technology at the community college: computer-assisted instruction, computer-managed instruction, distance education and televised instruction, and the role of learning laboratories and learning resource centers in housing and making available nonprint educational media. This final chapter reviews the most recent literature on each of these themes and concludes with information on how to obtain the documents and journal articles that are cited.

Computer-Assisted Instruction

One of the most comprehensive sources of information on computer-assisted instruction (CAI) at the community college is the New Directions sourcebook *Microcomputer Applications in Administration and Instruction* (Dellow and Poole, 1984). The volume includes chapters on the use of microcomputers as instructional aids in business, science, social science, writing, and adult and continuing education and an annotated bibliography of journal articles and ERIC documents describing CAI applications in classroom and tutorial situations.

Since the publication of the Dellow and Poole sourcebook, several articles and ERIC documents of CAI at the community college have appeared. Major themes in this small but growing literature include the importance of faculty development to successful CAI applications, the application of CAI in various subject areas, the use of video technology in CAI, and the efforts of some community college educators to compare the benefits of CAI with other modes of instruction.

Importance of Faculty Development. Those writing about CAI usually discuss its benefits. For example, Creutz (1984) maintains that CAI can increase computer awareness among students and thus prepare them for the growing number of jobs that require data processing skills. Brower (1983) points out that CAI can help learning disabled students by increasing motivation, providing instant reinforcement, and permitting them to work at their own pace in a noncompetitive environment. Netherton and others (1984) point to the usefulness of CAI as a means of individualizing instruction and, in some cases, of reducing instructional costs. For example, they note (p. 15) a TICCIT (Time-shared Interactive Computer-Controlled Information Television) program for music instruction "in which the student hears tones and identifies them as notes. It requires no piano, no studio, no endless hours of instructor time."

However, these and other authors are quick to point out that successful CAI implementation depends on large-scale faculty development efforts. Creutz (1984) notes that most commercially available CAI software is geared toward elementary and secondary levels, which means that college instructors must develop their own CAI materials. He also argues that implementation of CAI requires instructors to modify their teaching techniques and style. Netherton and others (1984) concur, noting that faculty at Northern Virginia Community College are granted release time to develop computer expertise and learn software authoring skills related to display specifications, branching decisions, anticipated student responses, feedback situations, and rules for communicating to the computer. Other faculty development efforts designed to familiarize instructors with computer technology and CAI implementation are described by Allison (1982), Peel (1984), and Wresch and Hieser (1984). All involve a considerable investment of time and money. But there is a consensus that this investment is vital to the success of CAI, for, as Koltai (1983, p. 7) maintains, it is the faculty "who will play a major role in deciding whether the new machines become tools of confinement or keys to unlock hidden doors."

CAI Applications. The literature describing actual uses of CAI at the community college is small, but it reveals the wide variety of ways in which computers can aid instruction. One way of using computers is to teach computer science and programming concurrently with other subject areas. For example, Capps (1983) describes the benefits of teaching computer science to students in vocational or technical mathematics courses. She notes that most vocational students prefer dealing with things rather than with abstractions, and she argues that the step-by-step process of programming, as well as the algebraic structure of programming languages, helps students to visualize mathematical concepts. Computers have also been used to enhance teacher performance in the classroom. Rorie (1983) tells how Dyersburg State Community College (Texas) integrated its campus time-sharing computer system with projection television sets that instructors can use as electronic blackboards. A third and more traditional CAI application consists of the computerized instructional programs that reinforce class subject matter through drill or simulation. For example, Edwards (1982) describes a CAI program designed to teach linear algebra, and McCall and Holton (1982) describe four CAI programs used in college-level mathematics courses to improve skills in the areas of polynomial functions, trigonometric functions, matrix algebra, and differential calculus. The fourth area of CAI applications uses microcomputer word processors to improve student writing. Newton (1984) maintains that students who use word processors are impressed by the professional look of their papers and that they develop a sense of ownership over their writing. He points out that word processing programs make revision a relatively simple task. These advantages are discussed by Levin and Doyle (1983), who report that several students at North Country Community College (New York) were able to improve their writing by composing papers on word processors at the college's learning laboratories.

CAI and Interactive Video. The literature on the development of computerized instructional materials often stresses the desirability of including video sequences in CAI programs. Tross and Di Stefano (1983) define this interactive video process as one in which the computer plays segments of a videotape or videodisc during the course of a computer-controlled tutorial. These authors describe the steps involved in developing interactive video programs and discuss the use of such programs in English as a second language and communications technology courses at Miami–Dade Community College (Florida). Another interactive video application is examined by Walton (1984), who describes the development of eight interactive microcomputer-controlled videotape training programs used to teach chemical analysis processes in the fisheries technology program at Peninsula College (Washington). Readers seeking a technical discussion of interactive video applications should turn to Oliver (1985), who details the various types of technology available and reviews the processes of designing, producing, implementing, and evaluating interactive video materials for vocational instruction.

The Benefits of CAI. Has computer-assisted instruction improved the teaching and learning process at community colleges? The literature rarely addresses this question. The need for time-consuming and expensive faculty development, the dearth of appropriate software, and the limited availability of funds for computer equipment suggest that CAI has yet to become a prominent mode of instruction (Simpson, 1984). Moreover, even when CAI is implemented, its effects may be modest. In their analysis of CAI and computer-assisted design (CAD) applications in vocational programs at three California community colleges, Charns and Porter (1984) conclude that, while computers served as a classroom diversion and socialization factor, they were not effective instructional tools. In an analysis conducted at Mesa Community College (Arizona), Lundgren (1985) compares the pretest-posttest gains of students in courses using CAI with students' gains in similar classes where programmed-text instruction was used. Students who used the programmed-text method had significantly higher gains than students in the CAI group. This finding prompted Lundgren to warn against the use of computerized instruction when other methods were more appropriate. Further research on the impacts of CAI at the community college is needed.

Available CAI Programs. The literature yields a small number of catalogues listing available CAI program for use at the community college. These catalogues include listings or descriptions of programs for use in agriculture and natural resources programs (California Community Colleges, 1984), drafting and electronics technology classes (Burlington County College, 1984), and forestry technologies (Martin, 1984; Watson and Scobie, 1984). Dimsdale (1982) lists and describes eighty-nine other teacher-developed programs in fourteen areas, including the physical sciences, humanities, mathematics, and health and commercial services. The small number of works listing available CAI programs testifies to the problems that community college instructors face in finding appropriate instructional software.

Computer-Managed Instruction

Computer-managed instruction (CMI) differs from CAI in that it uses the computer to analyze data on student performance and progress rather than as a drill or tutorial aid. For example, Roueche (1984) describes a CMI program called Camelot, which makes it relatively easy for instructors to provide students with feedback on tests and essays. In one application of Camelot, essay readers check off student writing errors on a form listing common stylistic and grammatical problems; the form is then processed by Camelot, which generates individualized feedback letters for students. This makes it unnecessary for the instructor to write detailed and repetitive comments on each paper.

The same principle can be applied on a large scale to track students through courses or entire educational programs. Of these large-scale CMI programs, the Advisement and Graduation System (AGIS) and the Academic Alert and Advisement System (AAAS) at Miami–Dade Community College (Florida) have received the most attention (Anandam, 1984; Anandam and DeGregorio, 1981; Anandam and Myers, 1976; Harper and others, 1981). AGIS is an on-line computer aid for counseling staff; it aligns student transcripts according to degree or graduation requirements and generates recommended course sequences for individual students based on their backgrounds and educational objectives. AAAS is used to inform students halfway into the term about their progress in individual courses; students receive information on their academic performance and attendance through the RSVP (Response System with Variable Prescription) protocol, which is capable of generating 26,878 different letters based primarily on information provided by instructors.

In addition to diagnosis, CMI has been used to facilitate flexible scheduling and independent study. For example, Fox Valley Technical Institute (Wisconsin) has made extensive use of computer tracking and support systems to facilitate competency-based round-the-clock education entailing short-term, flexible class schedules and individualized instruction. The college provides 6,000 full-time and 40,000 part-time students with more than 3,000 courses in ninety occupational fields. Students may register for classes at three-, six-, nine-, or twelve-week intervals, as soon as classroom space is available. The computer system used to support this free-form structure includes a student information and advisement system and a student accounting system that places students in classes and records the completion of course requirements (Fox Valley Technical Institute, 1984).

Distance Education and Televised Instruction

Distance education is the third major theme in the literature of instructional technology. The *Thesaurus of ERIC Descriptors* defines *distance education* as "education via communications media (correspondence, radio, television, and others) with little or no classroom or face-to-face contact between students and teachers" *(Thesaurus of ERIC Descriptors,* 10th ed., under the word *distance education).* Self (1983) and Zigerell (1984) describe the media technologies now used to facilitate distance learning. They include personal computers, videocassettes, videodiscs, teleconferencing, broadcast television, cable television, and instructional television fixed service (ITFS), "which employs a band of high frequencies to deliver education to sites equipped with the inexpensive equipment needed to receive the signals" (Zigerell, 1984, p. 12). Rude (1983), Holleman (1983), and Baltzer (1982) describe the combination of these technologies in multimedia approaches to distance education at, respectively, Chemeketa Community College (Oregon), the Peralta Community College District (California), and Rio Salado Community College (Arizona). Rio Salado is a noncampus institution, and it is especially dependent on these technologies. Besides print-based correspondence courses, it facilitates distance learning with cassette copies of radio and television courses in public libraries, audio teleconferencing, and cable television. The Rio Salado experience reveals that distance learning can be a success, provided that proper student and faculty support services are in place: " Students enrolled in telecommunications delivery courses and faculty teaching these courses require much more support than do teachers and students in the classroom because both students and faculty find themselves in very different roles" (Baltzer, 1982, p. 42).

Though distance education is facilitated by several types of media, the bulk of the literature is focused on television. Both Zigerell (1984) and Zigerell and others (1980) review the history of television applications at the community college and discuss research regarding telecourse students, and Zigerell and others (1980) discuss how colleges can get started in using televised instruction. Several ERIC documents describe the instructional television efforts at individual colleges or districts. Streff (1981) details a project undertaken by the Iowa Valley Community College District (Iowa) to provide information and instruction via cable television to persons eligible for Comprehensive Employment and Training Act (CETA) programs. Kennedy (1983) reviews a pilot project conducted at Cuyahoga Community College (Ohio) to conduct a section of a low-enrollment course, "The Psychology of Aging," in the main campus and the two suburban campuses. By using television to provide instruction simultaneously on several campuses, the college hopes to stem the cancellation of second-year courses due to low enrollments. Holdampf (1983) describes an associate degree nursing program at Howard Junior College (Texas) that, like the Cuyahoga course just mentioned, is conducted via videotaped lectures televised simultaneously on two campuses. Finally, Stover (1985) details the efforts of faculty at an unnamed Texas community college to develop a writing telecourse that meets the special cognitive and affective needs of nontraditional students. Each of the documents just discussed is useful in understanding the process of planning and initiating televised instruction.

Do telecourses extend educational opportunity to students who would not otherwise attend college? Clagett (1983) surveyed students enrolled in telecourses offered by Prince Georges Community College (Maryland) and found that for a majority of students (62 percent) lack of time for regular classroom attendance was very important in the decision to enroll in a telecourse. In a national survey of telecourse students conducted by the Instructional Telecommunications Consortium of the America Association of Community and Junior Colleges, Brey and Grigsby (1984) found that more than half of the respondents enrolled in telecourses because on-campus attendance did not fit into their schedules. Nevertheless, neither of these studies demonstrates that students currently enrolled in telecourses would not otherwise attend college. In fact, a statewide survey of community college telecourse students in North Carolina reveals that broadcast telecourses attract adult students who are very similar to those enrolled in on-campus courses (Julian, 1982). These and similar findings from earlier research lead Zigerell (1984) and Linville and Moore (1985) to conclude that instructional television has failed to attract large numbers of the nontraditional students who have hitherto been underrepresented in higher education. The literature leads to the hypothesis that, rather than leading large numbers of nontraditional student to enroll, telecourses have simply made it more convenient for the traditional college clientele to complete course work.

The failure to attract nontraditional students may be traced in part to the widespread use of telecourses produced for large, mass audiences that do not meet the indigenous needs of local service districts. Metty (1982) concedes that the high costs of telecourse production compel individual colleges to use materials distributed by the Coast Community College District (California), the Dallas County Community College District (Texas), and other large-scale telecourse producers. However, his experience with telecourse use in Alaska leads him to conclude that most of these materials need considerable modification if they are to meet the varying needs of local communities: "To not modify means that we insist that viewers adopt the vocabulary and orientation of the producers. This is de facto cultural homogenization" (Metty, 1982. p. 6). Purdy (1982) is not as critical of the telecourses leased out by producing and distributing agencies, but she does warn colleges to analyze telecourses carefully before using them, and she suggests seven questions that community colleges should ask about a prospective telecourse, including its compatibility with local curricular objectives. Further information on commercially available telecourses is provided by Purdy (1983), who discusses quality control in the production and design of telecourses, and by Zigerell (1983), who describes more than a hundred lower-division telecourses under eight headings: Adult Skills and Leisure; General Business and Management; Computers; Fine Arts, Humanities, and Foreign Languages; Health and Health Occupations; History and Social Sciences; Mathematics and Sciences; and Teacher Aides and Teacher Education.

Learning Laboratories and Learning Resource Centers

The literature on educational technology often centers on the role of learning laboratories and learning resource centers (LRCs) in housing and making available nonprint media for student use. The *Thesaurus of ERIC Descriptors* defines *learning laboratories* as "facilities with programmed or autoinstructional materials and the equipment required for their display" *(Thesaurus of ERIC Descriptors,* 10th ed., under the word *learning laboratories.)* LRCs, with their roots in the traditional college library, are defined as "areas within schools that provide services and equipment for the use of an integrated collection of print and nonprint materials" *(Thesaurus of ERIC Descriptors,* 10th ed., under the word *learning resources centers.)* These distinctions are blurred in the literature, which portrays both learning laboratories and LRCs as centers of instructional technology.

Learning Laboratories. Several ERIC documents provide descriptions of community college learning laboratories and of how they are used as an adjunct to classroom instruction. Shaw (1983) discusses a self-paced program in freshman composition at Brazosport College (Texas) that requires students to spend one to three hours per week in an instructional resource center with individual study carrels where they may listen to taped lectures that accompany the texts; both tapes and texts are prepared by the English faculty. Campbell (1983) describes the learning center at Dekalb Community College (Georgia), where one-on-one tutorials are combined with a variety of resources, including videotapes, audiocassettes, and programmed texts. Samuels (1984) details the operation and organization of a life science learning center that provides computerized instruction for students in the biology department at Los Angeles Valley Community College (California). Avery and others (1985) explain how microcomputer laboratories are use at DeAnza College (California) to provide mathematics students with computerized tutorials, and Mackie (1981) reviews an associate degree nursing program at Waukesha County Technical Institute (Wisconsin) that requires students to make considerable use of the institute's autotutorial learning laboratory. All these studies show how learning laboratories facilitate the use of instructional technology and help to individualize instruction at the community college. Students can use the laboratories to reinforce course material or to walk through an entire course on a self-study basis.

Learning Resource Centers. Most of the literature on learning resource centers is focused on the concerns of the librarians, such as the automation of LRC and library catalogs (for example, Ostler, 1984). But, LRCs are increasingly taking on the role of learning laboratories. The American Library Association (1982a, 1982b) issues guidelines on two-year college learning resource programs that relate to instructional equipment and materials, as well as to staff, facilities, organization, and management. In addition, Bender's (1980) national study of learning resource services includes a comprehensive examination of the use of media at LRCs to provide individualized instruction. More recent literature has focused on the LRC role in computer-assisted instruction. Bunson (1984) discusses one community college's plan to make microcomputers available to the entire college community through its media center. Terwilliger (1982), who believes that this is a sign of the times, predicts (p. 43) that LRCs "will evolve as a logical centralized location for CAI, providing access to terminals, maintenance at a single location, interdisciplinary staff training, and multiple supports through extended hours and flexible staffing." There is every indication, then, that the function of the library and the learning laboratory are being combined in LRC.

Finding Additional Information

The preceding paragraphs have reviewed a selection of the most recent ERIC materials on instructional technology at the community college. Additional material on this subject can be obtained through manual or computerized searches of ERIC's *Resources in Education* and the *Current Index to Journal in Education*.

Readers who want to consult the full text of the items cited here are referred to the chapter references. Items marked with an ED number are the ERIC documents. They can be ordered through the ERIC Document Reproduction Service (EDRS) in Alexandria, Virginia, or viewed on microfiche at more than 650 libraries across the country. Items not marked with an ED number are published journal articles, and they are not available through EDRS or in the ERIC library microfiche collections; they must be obtained through regular library channels. For an EDRS order form, a list of libraries in your state that have ERIC microfiche collection, or both, contact the ERIC Clearinghouse for Junior Colleges, 8118 Math-Sciences Building, UCLA, Los Angeles, California, 90024.

References

Allison, R. D. *Instructional Computing in the Community College: Project Report.* Bakersfield, Calif.: Bakersfield College, 1982. 48 pp. (ED 233 764)

American Library Association, Association of College and Research Libraries, and Association for Education Communications and Technology. "Guidelines for Two-Year College Learning Resources Programs (Revised), Part I." *College and Research Libraries News,* 1982a, *43* (1), 5-10.

American Library Association, Association of College and Research Libraries, and Association for Educational Communications and Technology. "Guidelines for Two-Year College Learning Resources Programs (Revised), Part II." *College and Research Libraries News,* 1982b, *43* (2), 45-49.

Anandam, K. *Effectiveness of a Computerized Academic Alert System on Student Performance.* Miami-Dade Community College, 1984. 43 pp. (ED 245 741)

Anandam, K., and DeGregorio, E. (ed.). *Promises to Keep: Academic Alert and Advisement [and] Statistics for the Winter Term. 1981-82.* Miami, Fla.: Miami-Dade Community College, 1981. 19 pp. (ED 215 726)

Anandam, K., and Myers, D. E. *RSVP [Response System with Variable Prescriptions]: Instructional Capabilities.* Miami, Fla.: Miami-Dade Community Collges, 1976. 57 pp. (ED 215 725).

Avery, C., Barker, C., and Soler, F. *A Microcomputer Lab for Algebra and Calculus.* Cupertino, Calif.: De Anza College, 1985. 10 pp. (ED 263 929)

Baltzer, J. "Variety Adds Effectiveness (and Spice)." *Community and Junior College Journal,* 1982, *53* (2), 26-27, 42.

Bender, D. R. *Learning Resources and the Instructional Program in Community Colleges.* Hamden, Conn.: Library Professional Publications, 1980.

Brey, R., and Grigsby, C. *Telecourse Student Survey, 1984.* Washington, D.C.:

Instructional Telecommunications Consortium, American Association of Community and Junior Colleges, 1984. 61 pp. (ED 255 258)

Brower, M. J. "The Impact of Computer-Assisted Instruction As It Relates to Learning-Disabled Adults in California Community Colleges." Unpublished bachelor's thesis, University of San Francisco, 1983. 52 pp. (ED 238 509)

Bunson, S. N. "Put a Micro Lab in the Media Center." *Instructional Innovator*, 1984, *29* (1), 29-30.

Burlington County College. *Curriculum Development for the 3-D Microcomputer Lab: Civil Technology, Architectural Technology, Drafting and Design Technology. Final Report of the Project.* Pemberton, N. J.; Burlington County College, 1984. 218 pp. (ED 250 512)

California Community Colleges. *Microcomputers in Agriculture: A Resource Guide for California Community College Faculty in Agriculture and Natural Resources. Update.* Sacramento: Office of the Chancellor, California Community Colleges, 1984. 227 pp. (ED 259 096)

Campbell, M. "Mastery Learning in the College Learning Center." Paper presented at the National Association for Remedial/Developmental Studies Conference, Little Rock, Ark., March 1983. 19 pp. (ED 247 592)

Capps, J. P. "Mathematics for the Technical Student: The Use of the Computer in the Systems Approach to Instruction." Paper presented at the New Jersey Consortium on the Community College Conference, Atlantic City, N.J., May 19-20, 1983. 33 pp. (ED 237 123)

Charns, H., and Porter, D. *Computers in the Small-Scale Construction Trades: Industry Applications and Education. Vocational Education Special Project, Final Report.* San Francisco: E. H. White, 1984. 118 pp. (ED 259 230)

Clagett, C. A. *A Review of the Telecredit Program, Fall 1976-82.* Report No. 83-4. Largo, Md.: Office of Institutional Research, Prince Georges Community College, 1983. 31 pp. (ED 229 091)

Creutz, A. *Academic/Instructional Computing in the Community and Junior College: Its Role and Its Institutional Implications.* San Diego, Calif.: San Diego Community College District, 1984. 10 pp. (ED 241 096)

Dellow, D. A., and Poole, L. H. (eds.). *Microcomputer Applications in Administration and Instruction.* New Directions for Community Colleges, no. 53. San Francisco: Jossey-Bass, 1984. 122 pp. (ED 247 990)

Dimsdale, J. M. (ed.). *A Guide to Microcomputer Programs in the California Community Colleges.* Costa Mesa, Calif.: Orange Coast College, 1982. 59 pp. (ED 231 408)

Edwards, S. E. "Use of Microcomputers at the Junior College Level in the Teaching of Mathematics." Unpublished paper, San Jose State University, 1982. 94 pp. (ED 226 698)

Fox Valley Technical Institute. *Computer-Supported Education at Fox Valley Technical Institute: IBM Application Brief.* Appleton, Wis.: Fox Valley Technical Institute, 1984. 15 pp. (ED 197 776)

Harper, H., Herrig, J., Kelly, J. T., and Schinoff, R. B. *Advisement and Graduation Information System.* Miami, Fla.: Miami–Dade Community College, 1981. 34 pp. (ED 197 776)

Holdampf, B. A. *Innovative Associate Degree Nursing Program—Remote Area: A Comprehensive Final Report on Exemplary and Innovative Proposal.* Big Springs, Texas: Howard County Junior College, 1983. 24 pp. (ED 248 402)

Holleman, J. J. "A Master Plan for the Use of Telecommunications for Instruction and Community Services in the Peralta Community College District." Unpublished doctoral dissertation, Nova University, 1983. 142 pp. (ED 242 342)

Julian, A. A. *Utilizing Telecommunications for Nontraditional Instruction in the*

North Carolina Community College System. Project Final Report. Durham, N.C.: Durham Technical Institute, 1982. 148 pp. (ED 224 957)

Kennedy, W. R. "Use of Live TV to Offset Low Enrollments in a Multicampus Setting." Paper presented at the Annual Meeting of the North Central Research Association, Ann Arbor, Mich., July 14, 1983. 13 pp. (ED 231 480)

Koltai, L. "New Technologies in the Service of the Learner: An Imperative." Paper presented at the National Conference of the League for Innovation in the Community College, Newport Beach, Calif., October 10-12, 1983. 16 pp. (ED 243 518)

Levin, R., and Doyle, C. "The Microcomputer in the Writing/Reading/Study Lab." *Technological Horizons in Education*, 1983, *15* (4), 16-19.

Linville, R., and Moore, D. "Telecourses and the Community College." *Community Services Catalyst*, 1985, *15* (4), 16-19.

Lundgren, C. A. "A Comparison of the Effects of Programmed Instruction and Computer-Aided Instruction on Achievement in English Grammar." *Delta Pi Epsilon Journal*, 1985, *27* (1), 1-9.

McCall, M. B., and Holton, J. L. "Integration of CAI into a Freshmen Liberal Arts Math Course in the Community College." *Journal of Computers in Mathematics and Science Teaching*, 1982, *2* (2), 35-37.

Mackie, M. K. B. "Autotutorial Anatomy and Physiology for Associate Degree Nursing Program." Unpublished report, 1981. 27 pp. (ED 209 482)

Martin, L. "Public Domain Microcomputer Software for Forestry." Unpublished paper, 1984. 24 pp. (ED 247 419)

Metty, M. P. "Policy Implications and Constraints of Educational Telecommunications in a Subarctic Region." Unpublished paper, 1982. 11 pp. (ED 222 216)

Netherton, J. C., Sasscer, J. C., Sasscer, M. F., and Wyles, B. A. "Computer-Assisted Instruction: A Decade of Experience in Humanizing the Use of High Tech." Paper presented at the Annual Convention of the American Association of Community and Junior Colleges, Washington, D.C., April 1-4, 1984. 31 pp. (ED 243 547)

Newton, S. S. "Computer Resources for Writing." Unpublished paper, 1984. 36 pp. (ED 254 262)

Oliver, W. P. *Videodiscs in Vocational Education.* Information Series No. 299. Columbus, Ohio: ERIC Clearinghouse on Adult, Career, and Vocational Education, 1985. 40 pp. (ED 260 301)

Ostler, L. "A Study to Determine the Effectiveness of On-Line Catalog Use for Ricks College Freshmen at the Learning Resources Center: Societal Factors Affecting Education." Ed. D. practicum, Nova University, 1984. 36 pp. (ED 251 153)

Peel, M. S. *A Comprehensive Program for Computer-Related Instruction at the State University of New York Agricultural and Technical College, Delhi, New York. Final Report.* Delhi: Agricultural and Technical College, State University of New York, 1984. 56 pp. (ED 259 783)

Purdy, L. "Here's How On-Switch Turns on Students, Too." *Community and Junior College Journal*, 1982, *53* (2), 20-23, 43.

Purdy, L. "Quality Control in the Design and Production of Telecourses." Paper presented at the Annual Conference of the American Association of Community and Junior Colleges, New Orleans, La., April 24-27, 1983. 12 pp. (ED 235 857)

Rorie, C. D. "Using a Time-Sharing Computer System in the Classroom: Large-Screen Projection Television as an Interactive Teaching Aid." *Technological Horizons in Education*, 1983, *11* (1), 121-122.

Roueche, S. D. (ed.). "Camelot: An Individual Information System." *Innovation Abstracts*, 1984, (14) (entire issue). 4 pp. (ED 248 923)

Rude, J. C. *Chemeketa Community College Telecommunications Network: A Proposal to the Chemeketa Community College Board.* Salem, Ore.: Chemeketa Community College, 1983. 44 pp. (ED 234 854)

Samuels, E. "Life Science Learning Center, Los Angeles Valley College." Paper presented at the National Conference of the League for Innovation in the Community Colleges and the Dallas Community College District, Dallas, Texas, October 28-31, 1984. 13 pp. (ED 253 289)

Self, C. C. "An Overview of Educational Technologies and Implications for Staff Development at the Community College Level." Paper presented at the University of Massachusetts, Amherst, May 1983. 36 pp. (ED 231 460)

Shaw, W. E. "A Self-Paced Program in Freshmen Composition." Paper presented at the Annual Meeting of the Southwest Regional Conference on English in the Two-Year College, Bossier City, La., October 6-8, 1983. 9 pp. (ED 244 291)

Simpson, A. H. *The Effectiveness of Computers in Vocational Education Instruction.* Flagstaff: Center for Vocational Education, University of Northern Arizona, 1984. 51 pp. (ED 254 676)

Stover, H. "Reaching Adult Learners Through Public Television." Paper presented at the Annual Meeting of the Conference on College Composition and Communication, Minneapolis, Minn., March 21-23 1985. 8 pp. (ED 257 104)

Streff, D. *Utilization of Cable Television to Provide Instruction and Information Services to CETA-Eligible Persons in Marshalltown. Project Report.* Marshalltown, Iowa: Iowa Valley Community College District, 1981, 75 pp. (ED 222 224)

Terwilliger, G. "The Future of Learning Resource Centers: A Partnership with Emerging Technologies." *Community College Review*, 1982, *10* (2), 41-43.

Tross, G., and Di Stefano, M. F. *Interactive Video at Miami-Dade Community College.* Miami, Fla.: Miami-Dade Community College, 1983. 10 pp. (ED 230 256)

Walton, J. M. *Development of Chemical Analysis Training Programs for Fisheries Technicians Utilizing an Interactive Microcomputer Videotape System. Final Report.* Port Angeles, Wash.: Peninsula College, 1984. 10 pp. (ED 255 649)

Watson, R. C., and Scobie, W. R. *Computer Software for Forestry Technology Curricula. Final Report.* Auburn, Wash.: Green River Community College, 1984. 21 pp. (ED 255 647)

Wresch, W., and Hieser, R. "Computers Across the Curriculum." *EDUCOM*, 1984, *19* (1), 20-22.

Zigerell, J. (ed.). *The Catalogue of Mass Media College Courses: A Selective Listing of Lower Division Undergraduate Courses Available for Lease or Purchase.* (3rd ed.) Washington, D.C.: Instructional Telecommunications Consortium, American Association of Community and Junior Colleges, 1983. 115 pp. (ED 234 849)

Zigerell, J. *Distance Education: An Information Age Approach to Adult Education.* Columbus, Ohio: ERIC Clearinghouse on Adult, Career, and Vocational Education, 1984. 84 pp. (ED 246 311)

Zigerell, J. J., O'Rourk, J. S., and Pohrte, T. W. *Television in Community and Junior Colleges: An Overview and Guidelines.* Los Angeles, Calif.: ERIC Clearinghouse for Junior Colleges; Syracuse, N.Y.: ERIC Clearinghouse on Information Resources, 1980. 46 pp. (ED 206 329)

Jim Palmer is assistant director for user services at the ERIC Clearinghouse for Junior Colleges, University of California, Los Angeles.

Index

A

ACCESS Consortium, 4
Adult Learning Service (ALS), 17
Alaska: learning resource centers in, 52, 54, 55; telecourses in, 4, 54, 89
Alaska, University of, and telecourses, 4
Albright, M. J., 51, 58
Allison, R. D., 84, 91
American Association of Community and Junior Colleges (AACJC), 4, 13, 17, 25, 50, 88
American Association of Higher Education, 4
American Council on Education, 43
American Library Association, 43, 46, 50, 58, 90, 91
Ames, W. C., 22, 28
Anandam, K., 35, 39, 65, 67, 69, 71-72, 87, 91
Anchorage Community College: learning resource center trends at, 52, 54, 55; telecourses at, 54
Annenberg Foundation, 17
Arizona: computer-assisted instruction in, 53, 86; learning resource centers in, 52, 54; telecourses in, 4, 54, 87-88
Association for Educational Communications and Technology, 43, 50, 51, 91
Association of College and Research Libraries, 91
Attendance, and performance, 39
Audiotutorial (A-T) system, 78-79
Avery, C., 90, 91

B

Baker, G. A., III, 29, 30, 32, 33, 38, 39-40
Baltzer, J., 87-88, 91
Barker, C., 91
Bay Area Television Consortium, 4
Bee County College, technology at, 59
Behaviorism, and telecourses, 6
Bellevue Community College, dial-access system at, 77-78
Bemidji State University, and telephone course, 61
Bender, D. R., 90, 91
Bloom, B. S., 75, 81
Bolvin, B. M., 77, 81
Brazosport College, learning laboratory at, 90
Breneman, D. W., 21, 28
Brey, R., 88, 91-92
British Columbia, telecourses in, 4
Brower, M. J., 84, 92
Brown, L. A., 8-9, 11
Bruffee, K. A., 5, 11
Bunson, S. N., 90, 92
Burlington County College, and computer-assisted instruction, 86, 92
Burton, J. K., 6, 12
Bush, R. W., 22, 28

C

Cable television, and copyrights, 44-45
California: computer-assisted design in, 86; distance education in, 87; learning laboratory in, 90; learning resource centers in, 52, 55; telecourses in, 4, 89
California at Los Angeles, University of (UCLA), Word Processor Writing Project of, 34
California Community Colleges, 86, 92
Camelot program, 35, 38, 86
Campbell, M., 90, 92
Canada: distance learning consortia in, 4, 25; satellite survey in, 14
Capps, J. P., 85, 92
Center for Learning and Telecommunications, 4
Center for the Improvement of Teaching and Learning, 39
Central Education Network (CEN), 15
Charns, H., 86, 92

Chemeketa Community College, distance education at, 87
Chester system, 77-78
City Colleges of Chicago: attendance study by, 39; learning resource center trends at, 52, 53, 54; telecourses at, 54
Clagett, C. A., 88, 92
Clark, R. E., 9, 11
Clark, T., 78, 81
Coast Community College District, and telecourses, 89
Coast Telecourses, 13, 17
Coastline Community College: and satellite transmission, 17; and telecourses, 4
Cognitive psychology, and telecourses, 6
Community colleges: challenges to, 21-22, 27-28; cooperation by, 21-28; and copyrights, 41-48; and low-achieving students, 29-40; multicampus, learning resource centers at, 49-58; and satellite transmission, 13-20; small, 59-64; sources and information on, 83-94; technologies in, 65-82; telecourses at, 3-12
Comprehensive Automated Learning Resources System (CALS), 26
Comprehensive Employment and Training Act (CETA), 88
Computer-assisted instruction: adapting to, 55-56; applications of, 84-85; benefits of, 85-86; and faculty development, 84; and interactive video, 85; for low-achieving students, 34-35; programs available for, 86; at small colleges, 61-62; sources and information on, 83-86; trends in, 53
Computer-managed instruction, sources and information on, 86-87
Computers: applications of, 65-72; collaboration for quality in, 68-69; and copyrights, 45-48; and human qualities, 71; and individualized instruction, 68; and leading and trailing edges, 66-67; and learning resource centers, 49-50, 51, 53, 55-56, 57-58; library networks of, 62-63; refinements in uses of, 67-68; responsibilities relegated to, 69-71

Consortia: regional cooperation through, 21-28; for satellite transmission, 17; for staff and organizational development, 30; for telecourses, 4-5
Cooperation, and change, 21-28
Copyright Act, 41-43, 44, 48; Section 117 of, 45, 47
Copyright Royalty Tribunal, 44-45
Copyrights: actions to be taken regarding, 46-48; analysis of, 41-48; classes in, 42; and computers, 45-48; and Copyright Royalty Tribunal, 44-45; and off-the-air recording, 43-44; renewal of, 42; summary on, 48
Cottingham, C. D., 59, 64
Creutz, A., 84, 92
Crowder, N., 57
Cuyahoga Community College: learning resource center trends at, 52; telecourses at, 88

D

Dallas County Community College District: learning resource center trends at, 52, 54; and telecourses, 4, 54, 89
De Anza College, learning laboratory at, 90
DeGregorio, E., 87, 91
Dekalb Community College, learning laboratory at, 90
Dellow, D. A., 83-84, 92
Demas, S., 47, 48
Descartes, R., 5
Dial-access system, 77-78
Dialog data base, 63
Dimsdale, J. M., 86, 92
Distance learning: and satellite transmission, 13-20; sources and information on, 87-89; telecourses for, 3-12
Di Stefano, M. F., 85, 94
Doyle, C., 85, 93
Dyersburg State Community College, computer-assisted instruction at, 85

E

Eastern Educational Consortium, 4
Easton, J. Q., 39

Edison, T., 74, 81
Educational Resources Information Center (ERIC), 83-94
Educational Testing Service, 29
Edwards, S. E., 85, 92
Elgin Community College, computer package at, 26
Empire State College, and telecourses, 4
Exxon Education Foundation, 34, 35

F

Faculty development, and computer-assisted instruction, 84
Fair use doctrine, and copyrights, 42-43, 46
Feasley, C. E., 5, 11
Finn, J. D., 53, 58
Fischer, M., 41, 48
Fisher, G., 67, 72
Florida, technology in, 59. *See also* Miami-Dade Community College
Fox Valley Technical Institute, computer-managed instruction at, 87, 92
Friedman, M. P., 34, 39

G

Georgia, learning laboratory in, 90
Gillin, P., 47, 48
Grigsby, C., 88, 92

H

Hagerstown Junior College, modular audiotutorial components at, 78
Harper, H., 87, 92
Havelock, E. A., 77, 81
Hecht, A. R., 57, 58
Herrig, J., 92
Hertling, J., 29, 39
Hieser, R., 84, 94
Higher Education Cooperative Act (HECA, Illinois), 22
Holdampf, B. A., 88, 92
Holleman, J. J., 87, 92
Holmberg, B., 6, 7, 8, 10, 11
Holton, J. L., 85, 93
Homer, 77
Howard Junior College, telecourses at, 88

I

Illich, I., 66, 72
Illinois: attendance study in, 39; cooperation in, 21-28; learning resource centers in, 52, 53, 54, 55; technology in, 57, 59, 61, 64; telecourses in, 4, 54
Illinois Community College Board, 22
Individualist theory, and telecourses, 5
Individualized instruction, and computers, 68
Information: cooperative sharing of, 23, 25-26; sources of, 83-94
Instructional technology: changes in, 49-58; changing use of, 77-79; classroom use of, 60; considerations in mix of, 73-82; cooperation for, 21-28; and copyrights, 41-48; criteria for, 50, 57; as delivery systems, 60-61; history of, 73-76; lessons for future of, 79-81; for low-achieving students, 29-40; promises and problems of, 65-72; satellite transmission for, 13-20; at small colleges, 59-64; sources and information on, 83-94; for telecourses, 3-12; and values, 76-77
Instructional Telecommunications Consortium (ITC), 4, 13, 17, 25, 88
Instructional Television Fixed Services (ITFS), 14, 17, 87
Iowa Valley Community College District, telecourses at, 88
ITV Center, 8, 11

J

Jefferson Community College (JCC), Recruitment, Retention, and Attrition (RRA) project of, 32
John A. Logan College, technology at, 59, 61, 64
Julian, A. A., 89, 92-93

K

Kelly, J. T., 67, 69, 71-72, 92
Kennedy, W. R., 88, 93
Kentucky: proactive preenrollment in, 32; technology in, 59

Klasek, K. R., 57, 58
Knowledge Network, 4
Koltai, L., 84, 93
Kurtz, E. B., 74, 81

L

Lake City Community College, technology at, 59
Landers, A., 77
LearnAlaska Network, 4
Learning Channel, 15
Learning laboratories, sources and information on, 89-90
Learning resource center (LRC): analysis of change in, 49-58; background on, 49-50; collections and services of, 62-64; and computers, 49-50, 51, 53, 55-56, 57-58; impact of changes on, 51; implications for, 56; and limitations, 59-60; and obsolete forms of media, 53-54; professional staff for, 57-58; at small colleges, 59-64; sources and information on, 90-91; technology and, 50-51; and telecourse utilization, 54; trends in, 51-53
Learning theories, and telecourses, 5-7
Levin, R., 85, 93
Liberal technical degree, proposed, 50
Libraries, computer networks for, 62-63
Linville, R., 89, 93
Literary works, copyright of, 42
Los Angeles Trade Technical College, learning resource center trends at, 52
Los Angeles Valley College, learning laboratory at, 90
Low-achieving students: access with excellence for, 29-40; articulation for, 35-36; assessment and placement mandatory for, 32-34; background on, 29-32; behavior management for, 37-39; conclusion on, 39; content-based instruction for, 36-37; exit testing for, 37; instructional prescriptions for, 36; macro-level model for, 30-31; proactive preenrollment for, 32; skill development for, 34-35
Lundgren, C. A., 86, 93

M

McCall, M. B., 85, 93
Mackie, M.K.B., 90, 93
McLuhan, M., 9, 49
McMeen, G. R., 57, 58
Macomb Community College, learning resource center trends at, 52, 53-54
Mager, R. F., 75, 81
Maricopa Community College, TICCIT at, 53
Martin, L., 86, 93
Maryland: audiotutorial program in, 78; learning resource centers in, 52, 54; telecourses in, 54
Media: obsolete forms of, 53-54; print, 7-8; standard equipment for, trends in, 52; in telecourses, 7-9
Mesa Community College, computer-assisted instruction at, 86
Mesabi Community College, technology at, 59, 61
Metty, M. P., 89, 93
Miami-Dade Community College: Academic Alert and Advisement System (AAAS) at, 38-39; Advisement and Graduation System (AGIS) at, 87; Camelot at, 35, 38; Comparative Guidance and Placement (CGP) at, 33; learning resource center trends at, 52, 54, 55; Response System with Variable Prescription (RSVP) at, 87; Standards of Academic Progress (SOAP) at, 38; telecourses at, 54; video programs at, 85
Michigan, learning resource centers in, 51, 52, 53-54
Mid-America, University of (UMA), and telecourses, 8-9
Mid-Illinois Learning Resources Cooperative (MILRC), 24
Minnesota, technology in, 59, 61
Missouri: learning resource centers in, 52, 54, 55; telecourses in, 54
Modular audiotutorial components (MATC), 78
Montgomery, H., 44, 48
Montgomery Community College: learning resource center trends at, 52, 54; telecourses at, 54
Moore, D., 89, 93

Moraine Valley Community College, criteria development at, 57
Multi-Users System of Interactive Computing (MUSIC), 55-56
Music, sheet, and copyrights, 43
Myers, D. E., 87, 91

N

National Center for Education Statistics, 29
National Education Association, 43
National Institute for Staff and Organizational Development (NISOD), 30
National University Teleconference Network (NUTN), 15
Nelson, S. C., 21, 28
Netherton, J. C., 84, 93
New Jersey, technology in, 59
New York: computer-assisted instruction in, 85; telecourses in, 4
Newton, S. S., 85, 93
North Carolina, telecourses in, 89
North Country Community College, computer-assisted instruction at, 85
Northern Illinois Learning Resources Cooperative (NILRC): analysis of, 21-28; background of, 22-23; benefits of, 24-27; bylaws of, 23-24; conclusion on, 27-28; success of, 23-24, 64; and telecourses, 4
Northern Virginia Community College: Alexandria campus of, 53, 55-56; faculty development at, 84; learning resource center trends at, 52, 53, 55-56, 58

O

Objectives, instructional, and telecourses, 7
OCLC network, 63
Ohio: attendance monitoring in, 39; learning resource centers in, 52; telecourses in, 88
Oliver, W. P., 85, 93
Open University, and student autonomy, 10
Oregon: distance education in, 54, 87; learning resource centers in, 52, 54
O'Rourk, J. S., 94
Ostler, L., 90, 93

P

Paducah Community College, technology at, 59
Palmer, J., 83, 94
Parsons, M. H., 78, 81
Peel, M. S., 84, 93
Peninsula College, video program at, 85
Peralta Community College District: distance education at, 87; learning resource center trends at, 52
Performing arts, copyright of, 42
Phoenix College, TICCIT at, 53
Piaget, J., 8
Piedmont Virginia Community College, and technical programs, 50
Pima Community College: learning resource center trends at, 52, 54; telecourses at, 54
Plato, 77
PLATO, 53
Pohrte, T. W., 94
Poole, D., 32, 39
Poole, L. H., 83-84, 92
Porter, D., 86, 92
Portland Community College: learning resource center trends at, 52, 54; telecourses at, 54
Postlethwait, S. M., 78-79, 81
Pressy, S. L., 57, 58
Prince Georges Community College, telecourses at, 88
Print media, and telecourses, 7-8
Public Broadcasting System (PBS), 13-14, 15, 17, 18
Purchasing, cooperative, 25
Purdy, L. N., 3, 6, 11, 12, 89, 93

R

Recording, off-the-air, and copyrights, 43-44
Reed, M. H., 46, 48
Resources, cooperative sharing of, 25-26
Rio Salado Community College, and telecourses, 4, 87-88
Roberts, A., 32, 39
Rorie, C. D., 85, 93
Roueche, J. E., 29, 30, 32, 33, 34, 35, 38, 39-40

Roueche, S. D., 29, 40, 86, 93
Rude, J. C., 87, 94

S

St. Louis Community College: learning resource center trends at, 52, 54, 55; telecourses at, 54
Salomon, G., 9, 11
Samuels, E., 90, 94
San Diego City College, learning resource center trends at, 52, 55
Saskatchewan, telecourses in, 4
Sasscer, J. C., 93
Sasscer, M. R., 93
Satellite transmission: analysis of, 13-20; background on, 13-14; future of, 20; goal of, 15-17; and private industry, 16-17; problems of, 15-16; survey on, 14; and Telecourse Channel, 17-20
Schinoff, R. B., 92
Scobie, W. R., 86, 94
Self, C. C., 87, 94
Shaw, W. E., 90, 94
Simpson, A. H., 86, 94
Sinofsky, E. R., 43, 48
Skinner, B. F., 6
Soler, F., 91
Somerset County College, technology at, 59
Sound recordings, copyright of, 42
Southern California Consortium for Community College Television, 4
Southern Educational Communications Association (SECA), 15
Southern Illinois Learning Resources Cooperative (SILRC), 24, 64
Staff: development of, cooperative, 26-27; for learning resource centers, 57-58
Stanek, D., 46, 48
Steinke, R. G., 21, 28
Stover, H., 88, 94
Streff, D., 88, 94
Students: access with excellence by low-achieving, 29-40; autonomy of, 10; telecourse attitudes of, 5
Systems approach: for instructional technology, 75-76; and telecourses, 6

T

Target group, for telecourses, 6-7
Telecommunications Advisory Group (TAG), 25, 27
Telecourse Channel, 17-20
Telecourse People, 13, 17
Telecourses: analysis of, 3-12; channel for, 17-20; consortia for, 4-5; and copyrights, 47; development of, 3-5; impact of, 9-11; impersonality of, 3-5; learning theories and, 5-7; media in, 7-9; responsibility for, 10-11; and satellite transmission, 13-20; at small colleges, 61, 64; sources and information on, 87-89; student attitudes toward, 5; utilization of, 19-20, 54
Telephone: as delivery system, 61; for low-achieving students, 32
Television: cable, 44-45; role of, 8-9. *See also* Telecourses
Terwilliger, G., 49, 58, 90-91, 94
Texas: computer-assisted instruction in, 85; learning laboratory in, 90; learning resource centers in, 52, 54; technology in, 59; telecourses in, 4, 54, 88, 89
Time-shared Interactive Computer-Controlled Information Television (TICCIT), 53, 84
Toffler, A., 65, 72
Tross, G., 85, 94

U

Underwriting, enhanced, and satellite transmission, 14, 18-19
United Kingdom, student autonomy in, 10
U.S. Department of Education, 25
Urbana College, attendance monitoring at, 39
Utilization: changing, 77-79; of telecourses, 19-20, 54

V

Vander Haeghen, P., 13, 20
Vaughan, G. B., 50, 58
Virginia: faculty development in, 84;

learning resource centers in, 52, 53, 55–56, 58
Visual arts, copyright of, 42
Voegel, G. H., 2, 41, 48, 73, 82

W

Walla Walla Community College, technology at, 59
Walton, J. M., 85, 94
Wandah, 34–35
Washington: dial-access system in, 77–78; technology in, 59; video program in, 85
Waters, G., 10, 11–12
Watson, R. C., 86, 94
Waukesha County Technical Institute, learning laboratory at, 90
Weiss, J. A., 21, 28
Wildman, T. M., 6, 12
William Rainey Harper College: learning resource center trends at, 52, 54, 55; telecourses at, 54
Wisconsin: computer-managed instruction in, 87; learning laboratory in, 90
Wresch, W., 84, 94
Wyles, B. A., 93

Z

Zigerell, J., 87, 88, 89, 94